Russian Esp

CW00503860

in the

United Kingdom

1935 - 1955

Edited and Introduced
by

Kevin Gorman

Acknowledgements

I would like to thank Dr Juanita Hoe for her support during the production of this book. David Grant for his kind permission to reuse the photograph of Wilfred Macartney. Paul Johnson at The National Archives images library for clarifying authorisation to publish from the file. Picture Acknowledgements

Every effort has been made to obtain copyright permission. The Editor apologises for any errors or omissions and would welcome these being brought to his attention:

The photographs of Guy Burgess, Donald Maclean, Melinda Maclean, Leopold Trepper, Hede Massing, French, Italian and English Communist Leaders in Milan (Harry Pollitt), and William Martin Marshall are privately owned by Schulmeister Publishing Ltd.

The following photos and images in this book add significantly to the context of the book because the photo and its historical significance are the object of discussion in this book:

Facism: Benito Mussolini and Adolf Hitler the "Berlin-Rome Pact" Munich 29.9.1938. ©Bundesarchiv, Bild 146-1969-065-24/CC-BY-SA 3.0

Soviet Minister for Foreign Affairs photo ©Department of Foreign Affairs and Trade website – www.dfat.gov.au

Theodore Maly, aka Paul Hardt. ©Schulmeister Publishing Ltd.

Edith Tudor-Hart ©Wikipedia

Walter Krivitsky redigitalised by Schulmeister Publishing Ltd ©Wikipedia.

George Whomack TNA - KV3/417.

Wilfred Foulton Vernon TNA - KV2/995

John Cairncross http://spartacus-educational.com/SScairncross.htm

Ernst David Weiss TNA - KV2/2230

Alexander Rado, Ursula & Brigette Kuczynski, Rudolf Hamburger, Allan Alexander Foote, TNA KV3/350

Norman Klugman redigitalised by Schulmeister Publishing Ltd.

Harry Smolka https://alchetron.com/Peter-Smollett.

Wilfred Macartney reproduced with kind permission from David Grant www.auxilieries.com.

Alan Nunn May ©wikipedia.

First published in the United Kingdom in 2019 by Schulmeister Publishing Ltd.
Copyright © 2019 by Kevin Gorman

The use of KV3/417 is licensed under the Open Government
Licence 3.0.

ISBN 9781799296768

Contents

List of Abbreviations

ARCOS	All-Russian Co-operative Society
B.B.C.	British Broadcasting Company
C.P.	Communist Party
C.P.G.B.	Communist Party of Great Britain
"D" Branch	MI5 Counter-espionage.
D.L.B.	Dead Letter Box
D.W.S.	Diplomatic Wireless Service
D/A.	Double Agent
F.O.	Foreign Office
G.C.H.Q	Government Communications Headquarters
G.H.Q.	General Headquarters (Military)
G.I.S.	German Intelligence Service (Abwehr)
G.R.U.	Soviet Military Intelligence
H.M.G	His (Her) Majesty's Government
K.G.B	Soviet Intelligence Service
K.I.	"Committee of Information" (Foreign Intelligence Service)
M.C.P.	Member of the Communist Party
M.G.B.	Ministry of State Security
M.I.5.	British Security Service
M.I.6.	British Secret Intelligence Service
N.K.V.D.	People's Commissariat of Internal Affairs
O.G.P.U.	Joint State Political Directorate
R.A.E.	Royal Aircraft Establishment
R.A.F.	Royal Air Force
R.A.S.C.	Royal Army Service Corps
R.I.S.	Russian Intelligence Service
S.B.	Special Branch
S.I.S.	M.I.6.
S.O.E.	Special Operations Executive
S.T.D.	Soviet Trade Delegation
UN.R.R.A.	United Nations Relief and Rehabilitation Administration

Symbols:

Cedric Cliffe used the @ symbol to indicate an alias name.

Editors Introduction

In 1997 the British Security Service (MI5) started releasing its early historical files to The National Archives. To date MI5 have released some 5000 files dating from 1905 to 1958. Within the released subject files there is KV3/417, which was originally designated SF441-0302-8/V1 *D3 Survey of Russian Espionage in the United Kingdom 1935 – 1955.*

KV3/417 was created from a suggestion between the head of Soviet counter-espionage James C Robertson, his deputy D.1 Courtenay Young and D.1.B Cedric Cliffe in November 1955. Their intention was to document the key events of the Anglo-Russian relationship over a twenty-year period. Cedric Arthur Lewis Cliffe a long serving Intelligence officer and a former Oxford Classics graduate who was well versed in Soviet tradecraft undertook the task.

Cedric Cliffe was born at the Hermitage, Bayswater London on the 2 July 1902. The only son of Professor of Music Federic Cliffe. Educated at Eton College during the First World War, and in 1918 he sat the Oxford and Cambridge School's Certificate. He was matriculated from Balliol College on 18 October 1921. At Balliol he studied the greats and received a first-class honours degree in 1921 and a Master's degree was bestowed on him in 1925. Cliffe was also the winner of the 1923 Gaisford Prize for Greek Verse.

On the 14 October 1925 he joined the Colonial Office as a Junior Grade of Administrative Class. In 1939, he is recorded on the London Electoral roll as being the BBC Overseas Programme Director and on the 4 March 1943 The London Gazette promulgated his service in the Royal Air Force Volunteer Reserve.

After retiring from MI5 sometime in the 1960s he lived in Cranham, Vicarage Road, Yateley Camberley and died on the12 June 1969 aged 66 years.

The written style of KV3/417 for an intelligence document is typically historical rather than analytical, as it was intended to be. This makes it easily readable. Moreover, the reader must remember that this document was written in 1955 and the use of grammar and hyphenation was different. Also, Cliffe occasionally uses old French words such as *connexion* rather than "connection". Furthermore, some country names have the old spelling such as Romania, which has been spelled "Roumani" and "Rumania".

The structure of the document was originally split into three parts, which Cliffe describes as "pre-war days of suspicion of Russia, the wartime honeymoon and the post-war period of disillusionment"

I have included *The Loose Minutes* that accompanied the document as these minutes record how the document came to the fore and they reveal MI5's intentions for it's distribution.

The *Foreword* written by Cliffe introduces the survey indicating its special reference to the "fluctuating value of Russian stock on the English market."

The first part *The Backcloth*, is an interesting potted history that recounts the rise in Russian espionage activity in the United Kingdom in conjunction with key world events. It starts in the mid 1930s with the rise of Mussolini and fascism and follows through to the British Communist support of the Spanish Civil War, which Cliffe states was a "turning point in espionage." Cliffe then sets out the rise to power of the Nazis and subtly points out the shift of focus from Communism to Fascism. Moreover, he highlights the United Kingdom's attempts to persuade Russia to become an ally and you can feel the disappointment in his words when he states that the Russians chose to "embrace the dragon rather than St. George," which was "humiliating as it was awkward" for the United Kingdom.

Towards the end of the war he throws up some interesting discernments in particular the Yalta conference and Roosevelts handling of Stalin and Alger HISS' possible impact on American Foreign policy. From 1945 onwards he takes us through the period when the "vodka flowed" in post-war Berlin through to the origins of the cold war and the events surrounding the Berlin blockade and the air-lift, which he states "was probably the biggest triumph of the western powers throughout the period of the cold war." Furthermore, Cliffe conveys a "personal angle" over the tragic death of Jan Masaryk[1], but he does not allude to what that personal attachment was. He then moves on to the political events of the Korean War and China's entry into the cold war and America's frustrations with it, specially General MacArthur's "chauvinism". However, more importantly Cliffe reveals the interception of "the famous letter of 6 June, 1952, from the Centre in Moscow to Canberra", which confirmed how fragile Russian relations where and how close the Russians were to entering the Korean War.

After the death of Stalin, Cliffe tells us about the prospective reforms under Khrushchev stating, "the iron curtain had been temporarily opened and a glimpse of a new Russia seemed to be appearing." The 1955 Summit Conference in Geneva held to settle unresolved disputes from Korea and the French Indo-China War, it seemed these talks gave everyone hope. As Khrushchev had accepted an invitation to visit the UK, there was talk of German reunification, the "Spirit of Geneva" was in the air, and it looked like Russia was coming in from the cold. However, Cliffe points out that MI5 was continually reading between the lines, and when Molotov turned up in the October conference with his "arsenal of Nyets" the "curtains were shut and darkness once again descended". It proved that MI5 was right to be cautious.

Part two *The Actors* is a who's who in the world of espionage during the 1930s, 40s and early 1950s. Throughout the document all the names of the *Actors* are capitalised for ease of reference. It is a fascinating insight into the professional "Russian stock", and the ideologues they recruited to engage in skullduggery. In the narrative of each subjects background you can sense Cliffe's respect for the bona fide well-trained professional spies like Paul HARDT and Henri ROBINSON, who he remarked, was, "experienced, clever and versatile". On the other hand you can feel his disdain for the rogue spies that came out of the International Brigade in the Spanish Civil War, such as Wilfred MACARTNEY, who were only in the game for personal gain. Throughout *The Actors* part Cliffe takes great care not to divulge what he calls "delicate sources". These were no doubt well placed human and technical assets. However, a lot of the pre-war intelligence was gleaned from the Russian 4th Department defector General Walter Krivitsky who was interrogated by MI5 in Jan - Feb 1940. It is also interesting to note that when MI5 released this file in 1997 a few of the *Actors* were still living.

The final part of the survey is the *Chronological Table*. The table compliments parts one and two with a time line of the key events split into two parts *General* and *R.I.S.* (Russian Intelligence Service). The *General* part being the key world events and the *R.I.S.* the key espionage events. Due to book formatting I have recreated this table as close to the original as possible. Moreover, the original document was referenced using paragraph numbers which was cross referenced with an *Index of Names*. Again, for the purposes of book formatting I have removed the paragraph numbers and replaced the *Index of Names* using page numbers.

Overall KV3/417 provides an interesting historical insight into how MI5 managed to connect the dots with UK Communist sympathisers and Russian networks, and what they did not know about Russian espionage up until 1955. It also provides us with a glimpse of how MI5 changed, especially after the GOUZENKO defection and the introduction of the "purge procedure" (negative vetting), in 1948. This is evident in the Chronological Table where apart from BURGESS and MACLEAN there were only two minor cases of espionage in the years leading up to the end of the survey.

Finally, anyone interested in the history of Russian espionage or the history of MI5 should find this book of great interest.

Kevin Gorman
London
XVIII.MMXIX

MI5 Loose Minutes

D.1

I have been thinking over the suggestion which you and D.1/ JCR[2] made for a D.1.B. history of Russian espionage in the United Kingdom during the last twenty years.

I think that this could be done without enormous labour and that it might be made into a useful and interesting paper, particularly if it was set in the historical framework of the changing atmosphere of Anglo-Russian relations over the period concerned (I could write this part largely out of my own memory).

I have embodied my idea for such a paper in the attached draft "Forward". May I have your views on it please?

[signed] Cedric Cliffe

D.1.B. Mr Cliffe.

I think it is a useful suggestion that the history of Russian espionage in the U.K. paper should be married in to the general political temperature of Anglo Russian relations. I also agree to the suggestion of dividing it into three parts.

If you are preparing a skeleton of cases, perhaps we could discuss it whilst it is still in the rough.

[signed] Courtenay Young[3]

D.1 17.11.55

D.1

I attach the draft of my historical paper on Russian espionage cases in the United Kingdom. It has been seen by Mr. Reed[4], as the expert on the old cases, who has raised only one point of substance - i.e. whether we should include anything at all about PHILBY, in view of the fluidity of the case. I feel, however, that, after all the publicity of last October, any reader of the paper would be bound to notice such an omission and would perhaps draw unwarrantable conclusions from it. I feel, therefore, that we must we must

1

put in <u>something</u>, but I have left the draft as bald as possible, omitting all matters of controversy between M.I.5 and S.I.S. and resting mainly on verbatim quotations from Marcus Lipton[5] and the Foreign Secretary. After discussion, Mr. Reed is quite happy about this. He has, however, suggested that it is perhaps unfair to leave the allusions to PHILBY in the chronological table cheek by jowl with all the proven spies. I am quite ready to out out all these allusions if you decide.

From the nature of the paper it can have only a limited circulation, and it was indeed originally proposed largely as a manual fo officers joining D.1.A. It must certainly not go to the Americans, since it reveals an alarming number of known spies still walking about free men. By the same token, it should not, I think, go to Commonwealth links, and I would prefer not to send it to S.I.S. The distribution should in fact, I suggest, <u>be confined to Head Office</u> and such of our own overseas posts as are likely to be interested.

[signed] C. A. L Cliffe

<u>D.1.B</u> 16 April, 1956

D.1

I have read the attached D.1.B. draft with interest. It is undoubtedly helpful in getting our present work into perspective, and when completed should be read by all D.1. officers.

I cannot see any objection to the reference to PHILBY in the main body of the draft. I agree however with Mr. Reed that the allusion to him in the chronological table should be removed.

The eventual distribution should in my view be confined to D Branch, and include:-

D,

D.1.

All D.1 Officers.

D.2/3.

D.4.

All officers in D.2, D.3, and D.4 should know that the document exists, and that they can obtain a copy from D.1.B. to read, should they wish to do so.

I was particularly interested in the reappearance of RADO. Do you think it likely that he might reappear as an active spy, and if so would any useful purpose be served by - for example - putting him on H.O.S.I.?

The same considerations seem possibly to apply in the case of TREPPER. Do we know enough about him to be able perhaps to reconstruct his probable appearance and with this, and a short summary of his history, at least to ensure that S.B. officers at the ports know of his existence and have a chance of spotting him should he attempt to re-engage here in his former activities?

There are one or two other historical characters who might be worth making some enquiries about, in order to see whether something might even now be gained by interrogating them - for example Charlotte MOOS and possibly Paddy AYRISS.

WILLIAM's holiday visit to Prague in 1950 suggests at least the possibility that he may have resumed his contact with the R.I.S. Do we make any arrangements for having a periodical check on the activities of such ex-spies - for example by asking Special Branch from time to time for an up-to-date report on their activities? Brigitte LEWIS is another character to whom this might apply.

I am not sure whether you know that MACARTNEY is personally very well known to Burt[6]. This is perhaps just worth bearing in mind, should we want the revive enquiries about him or his associates.

These points are only for your consideration: I should be glad, at your leisure, to discuss them some time.

[signed] J. C. Robertson

D. 15.5.56

D.1.B./CALC

Please see D.'s loose minute attached. Will you proceed with distribution as he suggests. I have replied to D. on the appropriate files as regards RADO and TREPPER but what are your views about interviewing MOOS and Paddy AYRISS? I see that MOOS was interviewed in 1940. Paddy AYRISS would appear to be a Communist so I should have thought it unlikely she would prove co-operative.

[signed] Courtenay Young

D.1. 22.5.56

Foreword

The choice of year 1935 for the beginning of this survey is purely arbitrary. There is really no logical reason for choosing any one year rather than another, but 1935 provides a tidy period twenty years to deal with and it was in this year that Mussolini's invasion of Abyssinia set the pattern of Fascist-Nazi aggression.

The first section attempts to outline, in a very sketchy way, the general world background to the particular events described, with special reference to the fluctuating values of Russian stock on the English market. Similarly the parallel lists of dates at the end should enable any given case of Russian espionage to be related at a glance to its proper historical perspective. The main story should in theory divide itself into three sections corresponding roughly to the pre-war days of suspicion of Russia, the wartime honeymoon and the post-war period of disillusionment. Unfortunately it does not always work out so neatly as this in practice, since many cases spill over into more than period. It is however always relevant, when considering the motives governing any particular case, to relate the date of its inception and development to the broad background of world events.

The cases are not dealt with in this paper in any great detail the object being rather to present a general picture of them in relation to their networks and to each other, with particular reference to any remaining loose ends and known but unidentified characters. Fuller write-ups of many cases, with details of all persons mentioned, can be found in D.1.B records.

The term "in the United Kingdom" in the title of the paper has been interpreted literally, and it does not deal, except in passing, with espionage cases in the Commonwealth, in British missions abroad etc.

Part One

The Backcloth

In 1935 Mussolini had ruled Italy for ten years and Hitler had for a year or so been the undisputed master of Germany. Fascism had thus had time to put on a cloak of respectability and, while it was still anathema to people who took their politics seriously, and more especially to those with left-wing views the majority of British people had come to accept the system, if not as an ideal form of government, at any rate as a suitable enough institution for wops[7]. The fascists had not seriously persecuted their minorities and (as the Duce's champions never failed to point out) he had at last cleared Italy of beggars and made the trains run on time.

In Germany, the Nazis were just feeling their feet. The Reichstag fire, which had taken place in February, 1933, had been staged and was duly exploited by them, and in the general-election of that year they gained an absolute majority in the Reichstag. Hitler thus became Chancellor (Prime Minister) of Germany, to which he added the office of President on the death of Hindenburg in 1934. It was not long after his advent to power before Hitler showed his hand in external politics. In July 1934 the Austrian Nazis, with his connivance, murdered the Austrian "Pocket Chancellor", Dollfuss[8]. But Mussolini, who had not yet been driven into the arms of Hitler and was in fact viewing the advent of rival dictator with a rather jaundiced eye, mobilised his troops on the Brenner Pass. Hitler took the hint; he withheld his support from the Austrian Nazis and Austria was reprieved for another four years.

Meanwhile Russia bided her time and concentrated on the fulfilment of her second Five-year Plan. It would not be correct to say that in this country no interest was taken in Russia, but such interest as existed was mostly confined to the specialists. Political memories, especially in England are very short, and by 1936 the Zinoviev letter[9] and Arcos raid[10] faded into the past, while the murder of the last Tsar and his family had become ancient history, together with the other atrocities of the "Bolsheviks". Russia, too, was a comparatively long way from England and the front of the stage was very fully occupied by the activities of Mussolini and (since more recently) of Hitler. Stalin, to the average Englishman, was a much more remote figure and as enigmatic as it was right and proper for a Russian to be. But this is not to say that anything like an iron curtain existed in those days. Any ordinary person could go to the Intourist office in London and buy a ticket for the boat from London to Leningrad and a fortnight's tour of Russia (conducted or non-conducted), and there was no need to be sponsored by a left-wing or Russophil organisation. On the whole, however, the people who took advantage of these facilities were mostly those who were already of a leftish persuasion or members of the pink intelligentsia. They went to Russia firmly expecting to find a red paradise, they came back full of stories of having found it, and were duly disbelieved by their "reactionary" friends at home. Apathy, rather than active aversion or admiration, was at this time the characteristic

6

British attitude towards Russia and its system of government.

The attitude of the British public towards Nazism was however by this time becoming a good deal more positive. Fascism, it is true, had acquired something of the dignity of an established institution as far as Italy was concerned (though the antics of Mosley and his thugs were enough to bring the name into contempt in this country); but the Nazis, even before they had attained supreme power in Germany, had made no attempt to conceal the way they were going, and the writing on the wall was clear for those with the wit to read it. Racial persecution, the establishment of a police state, the repudiation of international agreements, followed by external aggression as the circumstances permitted – Hitler had made no secret of his intention either in "Mein Kampf" or in his many stupendous examples of demagogic oratory. It was a generous re-action against this sort of beastliness and all that it portended which was to drive so many idealistic and thinking people in all countries of the world, and particularly the young, over to the leftward side of the arena and even beyond. When both Italy and Germany started their career of external aggression, those feelings hardened, and they continued to do so as the Nazi menace became more serious through the ensuing years. Refugees from Nazi oppression were made welcome and allowed specially easy entry into the United Kingdom. Many of them of course were Communists, but they were none the less useful, and generally reliable, as allies in the fight against the principal enemy of the day – Nazi Germany. Not every German Communist refugee was a FUCHS.

At the beginning of our period, however, these sentiments had not yet reached their full development. The beginning of 1935, indeed, does represent a period of equipoise and breath-taking before the catastrophic events which were to follow, with the flood of Fascist and Nazi aggression still held in momentary check, but awaiting its opportunity to burst out. By the end of the year the first barriers had been breached, and once this had happened events followed thick and fast. The year 1935 may thus be regarded as something of a turning point.

The first month of 1935 saw a plebiscite taken in the Saar to decide the future of the country; Nazi propaganda there had been intense, and the result was overwhelmingly in favour of Germany, which resumed control of the country in March. A few days later, Hitler denounced the disarmament clauses of the Treaty of Versailles (which the Nazis always stigmatised as a "diktat") and declared his intention of re-introducing compulsory military service in Germany. This was something of a bluff, for Germany was still disarmed, and decisive action at this stage by the other signatories of Versailles might well have been effective in stopping the rot. But nobody lifted a finger, and the pattern of appeasement was set.

It was Mussolini's turn next, and in October, on the look-out for a cheap and flashy victory, he invaded Abyssinia. The story of the imposition of sanctions by the League of Nations and of the controversies leading up to this decision cannot be told at length here. In the end, sanctions were imposed, largely as a result of British advocacy, but they were too little and too late. As a result, the anti-fascist powers had the worst of both worlds. The measures imposed were not sufficient to save Abyssinia, which was mopped

7

up by Mussolini after a campaign of six months; and, more important still, the decision to impose them had shown Mussolini that Italy, unless she wanted to be isolated in Europe, must look to Germany for friendship. Hitherto, Mussolini had been inclined to treat Hitler with some condescension as a junior dictator and as a sort of parvenu who had somehow made his way into an exclusive club. Now he was thrown into Hitler's arms, and there would be no more mobilisation on the Brenner when Hitler next turned his eyes towards the south-east.

The Abyssinian affair, though not of first-class importance in itself, had a great influence on subsequent events, because: -

(a)   It laid the foundations of the Berlin/Rome Axis.

(b)   It showed that aggression could be carried out with impunity and made to pay dividends in spite of all that the League of Nations could do. (Japan had, in a quiet way, already shown this in Manchuria five years previously; but Manchuria was a very long way off).

The results of the Abyssinian debacle were not long in making themselves felt. In March, 1936, Hitler had remilitarised the Rhineland, in defiance not only of the hated Versailles treaty but also of the Locarno Pact, which Germany had entered into without any sort of compulsion and to which Hitler had himself proclaimed his adherence.[11] In the autumn, he gave a formal out to his improved relations with Mussolini by establishing the Berlin/Rome Axis. (It was "Berlin-Rome" by now, not "Rome-Berlin"). A month later, he compelled Russia to think very seriously about the security of her eastern frontiers by concluding the Anti-Comintern Pact with Japan.

In the summer of this year, the Spanish Civil War had started. The policy of "non-intervention" was soon recognised for the farce it was, with Germany and Italy openly supporting Franco and Russia intervening on the Government side. The O.G.P.U. swarmed into Spain, and the R.I.S. talent spotters were kept busy among the left-wing volunteers in the International Brigade.

The year 1937, though a peak period for Russian espionage activity in the United Kingdom, brought comparatively few events in the broader political sphere, except for the fact that the anti-communist front was consolidated by the adherence of Italy to the Anti-Comintern Pact. In Russia itself, Stalin's great purge of the Red Army began, involving the liquidation of many of the early Bolshevik heroes and the consequent defection of REISS and KRIVITSKY.

By 1938 the tempo had accelerated again and the Nazis and their friends were on the rampage. In March Hitler occupied Austria, this time without a murmur from Mussolini. In September came the climax of Hitler's demands on Czechoslovakia for the cessation of the Sudetenland, leading to the ill-starred Munich Conference[12], which averted war for the moment but left Czechoslovakia, the key to Central Europe, completely without power of resistance against any Nazi aggression in the future. In spite of Chamberlain's optimistic declaration about "peace in our time", few thinking people believed that the respite afforded by Munich was anything but temporary.

In the following March (1939), Hitler annexed the rest of a defenceless Czechoslovakia, and Mussolini followed suit with another cheap triumph, this time at the expense of Albania, which he elected to invade on Good Friday. In the same month another loose end was tied up when the Spanish Civil War, ended leaving Franco firmly in power.

In May, the United Kingdom at last abandoned its policy of appeasement and gave Hitler the halt signal by entering into a treaty with Poland, his next predestined victim, under which the United Kingdom (together with France) guaranteed to come to Poland's help in the event of aggression against her. By this treaty, Great Britain had advanced her frontier, as it were, from the Rhine to the Vistula and stood committed in the extreme east of Europe. One result of this move was that Russia was suddenly brought back to the forefront of the picture as the arbiter of destiny in that area. It was essential for Hitler to know that he could fulfil his plans against Poland without Russian intervention and later, if necessary, switch his forces to the west without fear of a war on two fronts, the classic nightmare of German strategists. His day of reckoning with Russian communism could wait; for the moment all that mattered was to keep the bear quiet. Contrariwise, it was equally necessary for England and France to contrive that some proportion of vastly superior German forces (in particular their armour) should thus be pegged down on the eastern front.

The wooing of Russia thus began, and went on through the spring and summer of 1939, with the United Kingdom as the first most openly coveted suitor. The Russians were perfectly well aware of their own value and stood out for their price, including a guarantee of the integrity of three Baltic republics, which they feared might be used by the Germans as a springboard against themselves. The United Kingdom representatives in Moscow carried on their negotiations in classic style and with no very pressing sense of urgency; they could hardly bring themselves to believe that Germany was a rival to be treated seriously in the assault on Russia's favours, or that Hitler, who had built up his power by flaunting the Communist bogey could really be contemplating so devastating a volte-face as to fall into Stalin's arms. Thus the Anglo-Russian negotiations dragged on through the heat of a Moscow summer until quite suddenly, on 23 August, Molotov broke them off and announced the imminent conclusion of a non-aggression pact between Russia and Germany. It was Ribbentrop's greatest hour; the despised ex wine-merchant had carried off the heiress under the very noses of his aristocratic rivals and had left the western diplomats looking extremely silly – and not a little scared.[13]

It was later revealed that secret clauses in the Russo-German pact had provided for the partition of Poland between Russia and Germany and the recognition of Russian interest in Finland and the Baltic republics. It was not to be long before those provisions became realities.

The Russo-German pact gave Hitler the all-clear, and on 1 September he attacked Poland, with consequences known to everybody. It is not surprising that at this period the popularity of Russia among the British public should have sunk to a low ebb, since the role of rejected suitor is never an easy one to sustain with dignity or without resentment. The war against Germany had started in a leisurely way, and was indeed known as the "phoney war", so that during the winter of 1939-40 people in England had ample time to reflect on the blow to their security (and hardly less to their vanity) which had been delivered by the Russians when they signed the pact with Germany. Self-righteousness has always been one of the major English vices, at any rate in the eyes of foreign observers, and English policy has not always obtained a sympathetic audience abroad. But in 1939 we had acquired a morally unassailable position when we decided, however late, to call a halt to Nazi aggression; and the fact that, with the choices so clear before them, the Russians should have embraced the dragon rather than St. George was as humiliating as it was awkward.

Russia's stock was not in any way strengthened in the international market by her rapid grab of her share of Poland (which thus suffered yet another partition) or by the events of the Finnish war. It was an indisputable truth that the Finnish frontier lay only twenty miles from Leningrad, but the Russian claim that this fact constituted a threat to the security of the city was less easy to swallow. To world opinion this seemed rather like the proverbial mouse threatening the lions but at any rate, after the Finns had rejected certain Russian claims, the Russians declared war and invaded Finland. To the world in general this was a piece of naked and cynical aggression by a very great power against a small one, on a par with Mussolini's rape of Albania. To the left wing, however, and especially to Bloomsbury[14] and the professional Russophils it was a proper puzzler, and their emotions were, in the fashionable jargon decidedly ambivalent. On one side stood a small, very respectable, very advanced country, which for years had ranked as a model of up-to-date development on highly democratic lines. Finland had indeed represented the ideal of the progressive modern state to many thinking people who, while decidedly left-wing in their opinions, were unable to stomach the full dose of Communist theory. Over on the other side stood the big bully with the big stick; on the face of it it was the 1914 story of "brave little Belgium" and Germany all over again and just the sort of cause to rouse once more the generous, if misguided, enthusiasm which had sent thousands of young men, three years before to fight for the Spanish Government in the International Brigade. But it was not so simple when the big bully was Russia, the home of Communism and the guardian of all true doctrine, the Russia which could do no wrong, (It became still more complicated in retrospect when in June 1941, the Finns lost no time in climbing on the Nazi band-wagon and joining the Germans in their attack on Russia). However, in spite of this divided allegiance, there were many volunteers for service with the Finnish forces, some of them impelled by a genuine sense of fair play for "brave little Finland", others by a simple longing for action which the "phoney war" had so far failed to provide.

The "Winter War" was soon over. In spite of a splendid resistance the Finns never had a chance against the huge Russian machine, and the war ended in March 1940, with substantial cessions of territory from Finland to Russia. It was a significant token of world opinion, even if of no practical effect, when in December, 1939, Russia had expelled from the League of Nations, after refusing the League's offer of mediation in the Finnish war.

In the west, the German invasion of the Low Countries soon followed, culminating in Dunkirk and the fall of France. Between these two

10

events, in mid-June, Russia seized the occasion to occupy the three Baltic republics, which, it will be remembered, had been recognised as a Russian sphere of interest in the Russo-German pact. This action did not arouse any particular interest in the United Kingdom, where people had other things to think of at the time.

Russia, in fact, remained very much in the background, as far as this country was concerned, for the next year or so, until at one bound she came right back into the centre of the picture when Hitler, on the morning of 22 June, 1941, hurled his forces against her without declaration of war and in complete defiance of his hard-won non-aggression pact. He had of course, at this stage, no reason to fear a war on two fronts. He was the undisputed master of western Europe, from the North Cape to the Pyrenees, and Britain was still concerned mainly with the problem of survival and in no shape as yet to move into the offensive. Hitler needed the wheat and oil of Russia, and it seemed to him as good a time as any for a final settlement of his score with Communism.

For a moment, people in the United Kingdom were staggered by the audacity and unexpectedness of the blow and nobody quite knew what attitude to adopt. Obviously, in one way, it was all to the good that Russia, with her unlimited reserves of manpower, should be ranged, albeit unwillingly, in the anti-Nazi camp, but the memory of Russia as an aggressive Communist power was still fresh, and it was not easy to forget the humiliating let-down of the Russo-German pact, which had left Hitler with a free hand to carry out his plans. But the period of indecision did not last for more than a few hours. That same evening, Churchill went on the air and declared in round terms that anybody who joined in the fight against German aggression would be regarded as a friend of this country and would receive all possible help. Coming from Churchill, the life-long enemy of all that Communism stood for and the prime sponsor of anti-Bolshevik intervention in Russia in 1918, these words were decisive, and his attitude found general acceptance. Bygones were allowed to be bygones, and Russia was received as friend and ally. The second main stage of Anglo-Russian relations during our period had been inaugurated, and the C.P.G.B, which had hitherto been denouncing the war as an imperialist racket, discovered overnight that it was, on the contrary, a war of liberation and a crusade.

Whatever may have been the feelings of the English man in the street about Russia at the time of the German invasion, he soon became ungrudging in his admiration of the Russian resistance, culminating in the heroic defence of Stalingrad. These feelings were reflected in the measure of the assistance which soon began to flow, in many different forms, from the United Kingdom to Russia. The naval convoys battled their way round the North Cape to Murmansk, bearing supplies of all kinds, in spite of a great loss of lives and ships; far to the south a railway was pushed through Persia from the Gulf to the Caspian Sea and a back-door route to Russia was opened up; and in England Mrs. Churchill headed a public subscription fund for clothes and other comforts for Russia, which raised enormous sums. She herself later visited Moscow as an honoured guest. Thus during this period it became not merely blameless but almost obligatory for the patriotic Englishman to admire all things Russian. A mild form of Russomania set in: Stalin became, half mock

11

ingly and half affectionately, "Uncle Joe"; and on festal occasions the hammer and sickle flag hung beside the Union Jack and the Stars & Stripes from the most respectable windows in Wimbledon and Walthamstow.

Of course it was not roses all the way even during this honeymoon period, and the bear (as Churchill called Stalin) had his fits of the sulks, when he would demand the impossible in the way of supplies via the Arctic convoy routes and would not mince his words about the delay in opening the Second Front. The British public were naturally unaware at the time of these high matters; but they could catch the echo of Russian policy in the pronouncements of the C.P.G.B., which now not only supported the war but also kept pressing for the establishment of a Second Front, both in season and out, and defacing many a good wall and fence with painted slogans to this effect. By and large, however, considering the wide differences of outlook between the participants, the war-time association with Russia held together remarkably well. It was given a formal shape in a twenty years' treaty of alliance between Russia and the United Kingdom, which was signed in May, 1942.

By the end of 1942 the tide had begun to turn against the Germans; they had reached the limit of their advance in Russia and the allies had successfully landed in North Africa. This however, did not constitute a "Second Front", or like Stalin continued to press, within the meaning of the act. The Second Front in the event materialised only with the invasion of Normandy in June 1944, but from then onwards the allied advances, on both the Eastern and Western fronts, continued with only a few setbacks until victory was celebrated in May 1945. Berlin, it should be noted, had (like Vienna) fallen to the Russians, since the British and American troops had deliberately halted their advance from the west when they reached the banks of the Elbe, in deference to a previous agreement with the Russians.

In February, 1945, when it became obvious that the final collapse of Germany was imminent, Churchill, Roosevelt and Stalin had met in conference at Yalta in the Crimea for a discussion of some of the problems which would arise as soon as the shooting stopped. Yalta has been a matter of controversy ever since; how far, for instance, did Roosevelt (by then a very sick man) sow the seeds of future trouble by his rooted conviction that he, and he alone, possessed the secret of handling Stalin? And what part, for that matter of that, did Alger HISS, sitting at Roosevelt's elbow, play in shaping American policy?[15] In any case, coming events began to cast their shadows before them and, as ever, one of the first stumbling-blocks was Poland. Throughout the war, the United Kingdom and other western allies had recognised, at any rate de facto, the Polish Government in exile in London; the Russians, however, were now supporting the so-called Lublin Committee, which had been set up under their auspices soon after the liberation of that city, and which as soon as possible installed itself in Warsaw as the Provisional Government of the country. Churchill, who saw the way things were going, was deeply concerned about the Poles (who had, after all, been the cause of our entering the war); but the best he could achieve at Yalta was an agreement that the Provisional Government should be reorganised on a broader basis, by the inclusion of democratic leaders from Poland itself and from among the émigrés, and with a pledge to hold free elections as soon as possible.

The Potsdam Conference, which followed in July, after the defeat of Germany, showed a general worsening of relations between Russia and the Anglo-American partnership. It also marked the transition, in the United Kingdom, from the Churchill-Eden caretaker Government to the Labour administration under Attlee. If, however, the Russians hoped to find a Labour Government more complaisant to them than the Churchill administration, they were soon disillusioned by Ernest Bevin. As early as August, 1945, in his first speech in the House of Commons as Foreign Secretary, Bevin expressed the view that the governments which had been set up under Russian tutelage in Bulgaria, Rumania[16] and Hungary did not represent the will of the majority of their peoples, who had in effect only exchanged one totalitarian regime for another. This theme was to be often repeated in the years to come.

The "cold war" was an undeclared war, and it is not possible to define with any precision the date when the iron curtain fell. However, the occasion when this pregnant phrase was first used is clear. It was coined by Churchill in a speech at Fulton in the United States in March 1946. Churchill, of course, had at this time no official status except that of Leader of the opposition, but his personal prestige was still enormous and his words rang round the world. [text unreadable] proposals in the same speech for a "fraternal association" of the English-speaking peoples provoked an immediate and violent reaction from Russia, and Stalin himself denounced Churchill as a warmonger and compared him in unambiguous terms with Hitler.

It was therefore not surprising that only a measure of success was achieved by the Peace Conference which met in Paris in July, 1946, after several preliminary and more or less acrimonious meetings of foreign ministers. Before the Conference adjourned in October it had reached agreement on a certain number of points, but the all-important question of the treaties with Germany and the Austria was referred back to the foreign ministers.

Although in retrospect a steady deterioration in Anglo-Russian relations may be discerned throughout this period, signs of a friendlier spirit were not entirely lacking. In the summer of 1946, for instance, a British aircraft-carrier attended the victory celebrations of the Red Navy in Leningrad; a little later the editor of the "Red Fleet" was severely rapped over the knuckles by "Pravda" for belittling the achievements of the allied convoys to Archangel during the war; and Field-Marshall Montgomery had a cordial reception when he paid a visit to Moscow. But the case of the "Soviet wives"[17], with its emotional and sentimental overtures, had an exacerbating effect on relations which was out of all proportion to its intrinsic importance.

If any one incident more than another can be taken as marking the opening of the cold war, it is the Communist coup of January, 1948, in Czechoslovakia. The establishment of a purely Communist régime in Poland had been more gradual and had attracted comparatively little attention in the world outside. But the Communist assumption of power in Czechoslovakia, though still bloodless, was much more concise, spectacular and pregnant with omens for the future. It was not without significance that the Russian Deputy Minister of Foreign Affairs, Zorin, was present in Prague, for no very valid ostensible reason, during the six days of the coup.

A personal tragedy connected with the Czechoslovakian coup was the death of Jan Masaryk, the Foreign Minister, in circumstances never fully explained. Masaryk, both by his personal qualities and as the son of the founder of the Czechoslovak state, stood in western eyes for all that was most civilised and democratic in Czechoslovakia, and his death profoundly shocked the world. Even apart from this personal angle, however, the Czechoslovak coup hit the world as a revelation of Communist and Russian methods and caused a stronger revulsion of feeling than any other previous event since the war. As proof of this, the words of an English Labour intellectual are very significant. Referring to the Czech coup, Sir Hartley Shawcross said "two years ago, I was violently pro-Russian, I was on the extreme left of my party.... Step by step I have been forced more and more to the conclusion that the aims of Communism in Europe are sinister and deadly". Sir Hartley went on to contend that the Czech coup made the need for Western union additionally urgent. His words must have found echo among many thinking English people.

The second main turning-point in relations between Russia and the West came with the blockade of Berlin. By a joint declaration made in June, 1945, the four big powers had agreed on the division of Germany into four zones of occupation, with Berlin (which was geographically isolated in the middle of the Russian zone) enjoying an extra-zonal status and a corresponding division into four sectors. A quadripartite administration of the city as whole was set up, with access to Berlin from the Western zones guaranteed along defined corridors (road, rail and air). In spite of the obvious difficulties and Russian obstructionism from time to time, the arrangement worked no too badly. Each nation took it in turn to act as "host" for a month, and it was recommended to visit the Berlin Kommandatura (city administration centre) during the Russian presidency, when the food was excellent and the vodka flowed. British hospitality was decidedly more austere.

In June 1948, after a period during which traffic into Berlin from the west was partially obstructed on a variety of pretexts, the Russians imposed a complete blockade; all roads and railways into western Berlin were closed, and the city was thus entirely cut off from the western zones of Germany and apparently deprived of any hope of receiving supplies from that quarter. About the same time, the Russians gave notice that they would no longer attend the meetings of the Kommandatura, so that the quadripartite administration of Berlin was virtually dissolved.

It is not necessary to probe too closely into the Russian motives for flinging this drastic challenge to the West at this particular juncture, but it was clearly connected with the establishment of the West German Government and the Russian fear that this new unit would be added to the military potential of the West.[18] In any case, it was a challenge which had to be met, if the western powers were to retain any standing at all in Germany, and western Berlin could not be left to starve. The air-lift which provided the solution to this problem was a wonderful achievement of determination and technical skill. Supplies were flown into Berlin by endless chain of aircraft of all shapes and sizes, and the process went on continuously for a year. In May, 1949, the Russians called it a day and lifted the blockade. When the air-lift ended, the number of flights made into Berlin by western aircraft had exceeded 277, 000.

The Berlin air-lift was probably the biggest triumph of the western powers throughout the period of the cold war. Towards the end of the blockade western defence as a whole was strengthened and rationalised by the signature of the North Atlantic Treaty, which had the supremely important effect of ensuring that the Americans would retain a foot in Europe. In 1949, therefore, the western powers could hold their heads high. On the other side of the picture, however, the report of the first atomic explosion in Russia heralded the end of the western monopoly of the atomic weapons, and proclamation of the Central People's Government marked the final triumph of the Communists on the mainland of China.

The following year, 1950, saw the issue of the Stockholm "Peace Appeal" and the outbreak in June of the Korean war. Chinese Communist troops appeared in North Korea in November and transformed the face of the war, but there was never any evidence that the Russians participated directly in it, apart perhaps from a few liaison and intelligence officers. The Russian part played mainly off stage and in corridors of the United Nations buildings. The Korean episode was, of course, historic in that the troops opposed to the Communists there were fighting under the flag of the United Nations in what amounted to a full-scale war, even if an undeclared one. A meeting of the Security Council, which was held immediately after the North Korean invasion was reported, had condemned it as a breach of peace, and called on members to assist in causing the North Koreans to withdraw. This meeting of the Security Council, like several later ones, as not attended by Russian representative, who claimed that no meeting of the Council was legal under the terms of the United Nations Charter if it did not include the representative of "the Republic of China". The Russian case however, was weakened by the fact that they took part in Security Council proceedings both before and after this period, regardless of the fact that it was Chiang-Kai-Shek's nominee, and not Mao-Tse-Tung's, who sat on it as the representative of China.[19] It was, however, without benefit of Russian representation that the Council resolved to provide military assistance to South Korea, under an American unified command. The Russians contented themselves with accusing the Americans (outside the Council) of having jumped the gun and having themselves been the breakers of peace.

By the time China entered the Korean war, the Russians had returned to the Security Council, where they defended the Chinese case; and it was the fear of armed Russian intervention which was one of the motives that led the other leading western countries to take a stand against the proposal for an attack on the Chinese mainland, such as was advocated by General MacArthur. The stand was successful, and the chauvinism of MacArthur was to this extent controlled. But American feelings were again exacerbated by the Russians when the latter supported the Communists in their charges of germ warfare and then blocked the appointment of the impartial Commission of Enquiry which was proposed by the Americans. So the fighting in Korea dragged on until, after long and tedious negotiations, an armistice was signed in July, 1953. The Korean episode had not actually brought the armed forces of the Soviet into conflict with western nations, but tension had been very high, and war between Russia and the west had been by no means impossible, (The famous letter of 6 June, 1952, from the Centre in Moscow to Canberra showed that the Russians also realised this possibility).[20] It had also never been open to any doubt in Korea that Russia, while still remaining a member of the United Nations, had ranged the whole weight of her influence on the side of those forces which had been branded by the United Nations as the aggressors.

In March, 1953, while the Korean war was still on, the death of Stalin removed a great monolith which had dominated the scene during the whole period under review. With the internal manoeuvres of the committee of lesser who men succeeded him we are not concerned here. It is enough to record that Beriya (a fellow – Georgian of Stalin) was arrested in June, 1953, and executed, with several of his associates, in December. From then on, any past errors in Russian policy (such as the break with Tito in 1948) could conveniently and posthumously be laid on the shoulders of Beriya, who was now discovered to have been a traitor in the pay of the imperialist warmongers.[21] Malenkov[22] fell from grace in February 1954, but contrived to retain his life, with a mediocre and decorative place in the hierarchy – at any rate until the time of writing this. Khrushchev and Bulganin were left as the masters of Russia, with Zhukov, a genuine soldier, in the important post of Minister of Defence.

When the smoke cleared away after Stalin's death and the removal of Beriya, a generally more relaxed and almost genial atmosphere began to become noticeable, both in external policy and in the internal government of Russia, where the housewife was promised more pots and pans and there was a lightening of the literary and other censorships. The most notable illustration of this new attitude during 1954 was the behavior of the Russian delegation at the Geneva Conference on Indo-China, which was more co-operative and cordial than it had been at any such meeting since the war. This conference was also highly significant as being the first occasion on which France and Britain (but not America) had sat down at a table on equal terms with the representatives of Communist China.

The Petrov defection in April, 1954 had led to the stock allegations on Russian side in an attempt to discredit him, and shortly afterwards to the withdrawal of their diplomatic mission in Australia, which was undertaken spontaneously by the Russians and not at the request of the Commonwealth Government. By and large, however, the relations of the Russians with western powers continued to improve during this period, and the climax came with the long-awaited "Summit" Conference at Geneva in July, 1955.

Although Geneva settled nothing definite, but left all the outstanding knotty problems, such as the future of Germany, to be dealt with by future meetings of foreign ministers, it ended in an atmosphere of good will all round. There was talk everywhere of the lifting of the iron curtain and of the end of the cold war, and the "Spirit of Geneva" came to mean something other than gin. There was to be fee travel between the east and west (and not only in conducted parties of selected individuals), trade was to be expanded and freed from irksome restrictions, and the jamming of western wireless stations would soon be a thing of the past. Then the Prime Minister announced in the House of Commons that Bulganin and Khrushchev had accepted an invitation to visit England in the spring of 1956, his statement was greeted with rousing cheers from all parties.

For a time all appeared to be well. Bulganin gave an arcadian garden party to the diplomatic corps at his little place in the country; the Ambassador Malik switched on the illuminations at Blackpool; there was a successful exchange of naval visits between Leningrad and Portsmouth; a team of Russian dancers was well received at Earl's Court and a British company invited to play "Hamlet" in Moscow. But to those who read between the lines there was food for thought in a very outspoken statement by Khrushchev and it soon became clear that the Russians had every intention of using Geneva for their own ends. They launched a determined and successful diplomatic offensive in the Middle east; there were inspired whispers that the conscription period in the United Kingdom could now be shortened and that MI5 had outlived its purpose; and Russian intelligence officers were soon making clear their hopes that the Geneva spirit, while acting as an opiate to the security services, would at the same time serve as a stimulant to the zeal of their well-wishers.

When the foreign ministers met (again at Geneva) in November, it soon became evident that the geniality of July had not survived the nip of autumn. Molotov arrived armed with a newly-furbished arsenal of "Nyets", and the Conference broke up having accomplished precisely nothing; it had failed to achieve agreement even on such minor points as wireless jamming, let alone the major problems of German reunification or disarmament. The cold war was on again and the iron curtain had once more descended. True, the "Hamlet" company did visit Moscow and was generously, if not ecstatically, acclaimed; but by the end of 1955 Russia gleefully announced the explosion of the biggest hydrogen bomb ever; she was claiming (in defiance of occupation statue) that East Germany had sovereignty over the eastern sector of Berlin; Bulganin and Khrushchev had completed a tour of India and Burma where they were rapturously received and took every opportunity of blackguarding and vilifying the western powers, with special reference to Great Britain. As the Russian leaders do little without premeditation, it was widely assumed that Khrushchev's buffooneries had their purpose, and that the intention behind them was to provoke H.M.G. into withdrawing the invitation to visit England and thus lay upon British shoulders the responsibility for renewing the cold war. In this manoeuvre, at any rate, the Russians were unsuccessful.

17

Part Two

The Actors

PAUL HARDT

One of the leading figures amongst the great pre-war "internationals"[23] was Theodore MALY[24], more usually known by his alias Paul HARDT who was responsible for the O.G.P.U. network in England at any rate from mid 1935 to mid 1937. By a rather curious arrangement KRIVITSKY, as head of the parallel G.R.U. network in western Europe, had certain supervisory powers over HARDT and his work, but for practical day-to-day purposes HARDT controlled the network. As it happened KRIVITSKY and HARDT were personal friends, and much of what we know about HARDT rests on the evidence of KRIVITSKY, who in general has proved an extremely trustworthy witness. In HARDT's case there is also a good deal of collateral evidence to confirm him.

HARDT was a figure out of a Phillip Oppenheim[25] novel - six foot four in height, ex-monk, ex-cavalry officer and lady-killer. A Hungarian by birth he had been taken prisoner by the Russians in the 1914 war, while acting as regimental chaplain, and had turned Communist. When he met Hede MASSING in Paris in 1933 he had already been operating for a number of years, and was an important Russian agent. HARDT availed himself freely of the ease of travel and lack of restrictions on current etc., which made life so easy for the "internationals" of that period, and he was equally at home in most of the capitals of western Europe. It was in those days no trouble at all for a head agent to run a network in England from any of the neighbouring continental countries, and thus to satisfy the condition, postulated by FOOTE as a general rule, that an illegal resident should never operate against the country in which he is stationed. The year 1935 actually found HARDT established in Amsterdam, but traces of him continually appear during the ensuing two years both in London and Paris. Based in Amsterdam, HARDT paid visits to England under cover of representing GADA, a properly constituted firm of rag and paper merchants, with headquarters in Amsterdam and an office in London. GADA was in fact one of a number of such firms, all enjoying a regular legitimate trade and many of them with wide international ramifications, which during this period were funded and used for cover purposes by both branches of the R.I.S.

In June 1937, HARDT and his wife left their London flat in a hurry, telling the porter that they would return shortly. They travelled to Paris, where HARDT's friend KRIVITSKY, tried to dissuade him from returning to Moscow, since Stalin's purge was at that time operating in full force. HARDT however, after presiding over a meeting of O.G.P.U. agents in Paris sailed from Le Havre for Russia at the end of July. His fate is uncertain. One account has it that he was shot as Trotskyist, but KRIVITSKY was told in 1938 that he was still alive, and letters purporting to come from him were received in July, 1938. He was also reported by a reliable witness to have been seen in England in 1939. On the whole, however, the likelihood is that he

19

was purged. The re-appearance of the long-vanished RADO at the end of 1955 certainly suggests that unconfirmed accounts of leading agents having been purged should be received with considerable caution, but in HARDT's case his exceptional height would be impossible to disguise, and would appear to make him unsuitable for re-infiltration into the west.

Among the English spies controlled by HARDT were J.H KING (whom he took over from PIECK), Percy GLADING and the "Imperial Council Source" in the Foreign Office, now believed to have ben MACLEAN. These cases are dealt with separately. It was stated by KRIVITSKY that early in 1937 HARDT recruited a young English journalist of good family to go to Spain (and the throes of the Civil War) and arrange for the assassination of Franco. A number of candidates for this vacancy have from time to time been put forward, but there has never been a firm identification of this man.[26]

Brian GOOLD-VERSHOYLE

One minor member of HARDT's network in the United Kingdom was Brian GOOLD-VERSCHOYLE, whose story might be taken as a cautionary tale against playing with fire. This hapless young man was an Irishman of good family and education, born in 1912, and a radio engineer by profession. VERSCHOYLE was a Communist of the idealistic type, who had joined the party in his early manhood and who paid a tourist visit to Russia, the land of his dreams. His brother was married to a Russian woman, Olga DEIROVA, who was a member of the O.G.P.U. The recruitment of the starry-eyed young Brian by his sister-in-law cannot have been a difficult matter, and in 1936 he again went to Moscow, this time for a course at the radio school. On his return to England he acted as a courier for HARDT, who had taken over from PIECK the control of KING, collecting KING's Foreign Office documents from a house rented for the purpose and conveying them to HARDT. According to KRIVITSKY, VERSCHOYLE believed that he was being used for purely political (i.e. Communist Party) work and was deeply shocked when he discovered by chance he had been handling secret Foreign Office papers.

This discovery was not enough to shatter his ideals, however, and early in 1937 he went to Spain, where the civil war was raging, as a radio technician on the Government side. Here he had further shocks awaiting him and found himself horrified by the methods of the O.G.P.U. agents who had swarmed into Spain and were busy liquidating all members of the Government forces who were not prepared to play the Communist game. VERSCHOLYLE was then injudicious enough to express his criticisms of the O.G.P.U. aloud. As a result he was lured on board a Soviet ship visiting Barcelona on the pretext that its radio transmitter needed repair; once on board he was seized and transported to Russia. In 1941 he was reported to be a prisoner on an arctic island[27] and in 1941 he was officially stated by the Soviet Ministry of Foreign Affairs to have been killed on a railway journey during a German air-raid. His brother Hamilton (who used GOOLD only as a surname) returned to Ireland during the war, though without his Russian wife.

The following persons were also associated, in one capacity or another with the HARDT network:-

Paddy AYRISS

Born in 1903 and an active Communist since 1927, she had worked in Moscow and Berlin before becoming involved with a Danish spy-ring which was exposed in 1935 but of which she denied all knowledge. In 1936 she took a job at the Soviet Embassy in London, later becoming secretary to MAISKY, the Ambassador, and was believed to act as intermediary between the Embassy, Glading, HARDT and the BRANDES (q.v). She later became closely associated with Simon KREMER, secretary to the Military Attaché, who was FUCHS' first controller. In 1940 she married Douglas GARMAN, a prominent member of the British Communist Party, who retired to the country to write in 1950. In 1952 she was heard of in Prague, Moscow and China.

Willy BRANDES

A Rumanian by birth, who succeeded Paul HARDT as controller of the GLADING organisation, probably using the name STEVENS while in the United Kingdom. He has not been heard of since he left London for Paris in 1937.

Edith TUDOR-HART, nee SUSCHITZKY

An Austrian jewess, born in 1908 and expert photographer. In 1932/33 she is known to have worked for the R.I.S. in Italy and Austria, where she ran a photographic studio as cover. In 1933 she married Alexander TUDOR-HART, with whom she had previously lived, and thus obtained British nationality. Having returned to England and set up a studio she became implicated in the GLADING case when it was discovered that the invoices for his equipment had been sent to her studio. She was also friendly with Charlotte MOOS, the mistress of Brian GOOLD-VERSCHOYLE. In 1947 she was again in communication with Arpad HAAS with whom she had worked for the R.I.S. in Vienna in 1932/33. She still runs a photographic business in St John's Wood, and remains a member of the Communist Party, which she joined in 1927.[28]

Charlotte MOOS

A German Jewess, born in 1909, she was the mistress of Brian GOOLD-VERSCHOYLE and a close friend of Edith TUDOR-HART. KRIVITSKY was convinced that she was an O.G.P.U. agent. She was interned in England in 1940, but was released in 1941, and naturalised in 1947. When last heard of she was living with her husband in Durham.

"JOHN" or "JOHNNY"

This was the cover-name of a contact of Paul HARDT, who in 1937 or 1938 stole blue-prints from a war production factory where he worked. The defector ORLOV stated that he was asked to provide accommodation in Spain for JOHNNY when Scotland Yard got on his tail and he had to flee the country. This JOHNNY may be identical with a JOHN who was member of the Henri ROBINSON network and provided drawings, etc., from an aero-engine factory near Manchester about the same time, but neither man has been satisfactorily identified.

Henri Christian PIECK

Another leading figure in this network was Henri Christian PIECK, a Dutch artist, cartoonist and architect, who was born in 1895. He visited Russia a number of times during the twenties and in 1932 he was recruited for the R.I.S. by the famous illegal, Ignace REISS, to whom he had been introduced by a Dutch Communist. PIECK's first major assignment was in Geneva, where he was sent with the deliberate purpose of cultivating members of the British Foreign Office staff, who were regularly there in connexion with League of Nations work. PIECK was allowed plenty of money and he lived in Geneva in an open-handed way, so that, with his genuine artistic ability and exceptional charm and intelligence, he had little difficulty in making himself acceptable to British officials and journalists in general and to Foreign Office staff in particular.

PIECK, however, did not rush matters. Having made five or six personal friends among the Foreign Office employees he invited two or three them to stay with him at The Hague, where he entertained them lavishly and lent money to the needy ones. His choice for an agent finally fell on John Herbert KING (q.v.), with whose financial circumstances he had fully acquainted himself, and in the summer of 1935 he visited London and recruited KING. Like all good "internationals" of the period, he travelled extensively, and in the year 1935 he is recorded as having visited England alone no less than fifteen times, apart from odd trips to France, Spain, Germany, etc.

Early in 1936 PIECK was succeeded in his control of KING by Paul HARDT (q.v.), who was a close personal friend of his. It is believed that PIECK's withdrawal on the orders of KRIVITSKY was due to a suggestion that he had become of interest to the British Security Service (KRIVITSKY, it will be remembered, though himself head of the G.R.U. organisation in Western Europe, had certain supervisory powers over the OGPU networks in that area). At the same time PIECK ceased to be controlled by his former superior "HANS"[29], a Soviet national possibly identical with OLDHAM's former controller, GALLENI, who was another user of the GADA cover employed by Paul HARDT. At any rate it was clear to PIECK from the briefs he received that HANS knew a good deal about the workings of the Foreign Office.

PIECK's later history has little to do with the United Kingdom, since on leaving England he was directed to espionage against Germany. In 1937 he was much affected by the decision of Ignace REISS to break with the R.I.S. as a result of Stalin's purges. When REISS defected, PIECK was ordered by KRIVITSKY to shoot him, but refused; and when KRIVITSKY himself defected shortly afterwards, as a result of REISS's death at other hands, PIECK lost contact with the R.I.S. He was interned by the Germans during the war, but survived and went back to live in The Hague after the war.

It has been said that PIECK was recalled from the United Kingdom in 1936 because of a suspicion that he had aroused the interest of the British. This idea seems to have been put into PIECK's mind by W.J. HOOPER[30], a former employee of the Passport Control Office at The Hague, who is known to have worked also for the G.I.S. and the R.I.S. in Holland before the war. HOOPER was a personal friend of PIECK, to whom he always looked in times of trouble, which with him were frequent, but this did not prevent HOOPER from reporting PIECK to M.I.6. at a time when he HOOPER, was desperately anxious to return to M.I.6. service. During the war he did in fact work for M.I.6., and later worked for M.I.5., until his story of his former employment with he G.I.S. became known. In 1950, HOOPER was again living in Holland and again sponging on PIECK.

John Herbert KING

John Herbert KING was a gift to the R.I.S. A man of nearly fifty when he first came into contact with them, he was only a temporary cypher clerk in the Communications Department of the Foreign Office. Being established, he had no position to look forward to; he was a gambler and was living well above his income, since he had a wife (from whom he was separated) to maintain, as well as a mistress, Helen WILKIE, to whom he was devoted. He also had a taste for whiskey.

To make things simpler for the R.I.S., KING's name had been one of those given to his controller by Ernest OLDHAM, an earlier Foreign Office spy, before he committed suicide in 1933. KING was therefore already a marked man when, in the course of an official mission to Geneva, he was introduced by a colleague to Henri PIECK (q.v.), who was living a stylish, open-handed life in Geneva with the precise object of making contacts such as KING. PIECK was also constantly travelling to and from the United Kingdom and on the Continent, and during one of his visits to England in 1935 he clinched the recruitment of KING. It is open to doubt whether KING, in his anxiety for financial security for himself and Helen Wilkie, would have been able to resist a straight invitation to work for the Russians, but in fact the proposition made by PIECK was not so quite crude. PIECK's story was that he was working for a big banker in The Hague, who would be able to make very profitable deals if he could get advance information about the trend of international affairs. PIECK offered to share with KING profits of such deals if he would hand over copies of the telegrams coming into the Foreign Office from British embassies and legations in various parts of the world, which contained informed forecast of the likely course of political events.

King apparently accepted PIECK's story and agreed to collaborate. The telegrams he passed over were not of high secrecy, and KING afterwards claimed that he had not in any way endangered the security of the state by his action. The telegrams which he handed over were always decoded copies, and KING steadfastly maintained that he never passed any cypher tables, although he undoubtedly had the opportunity to do so and was in fact asked for such material by PIECK's successor. The telegrams handed over were for retention and did not have to be photographed. KING did, however, know that PIECK did photography, as he had seen the apparatus when he visited PIECK's office in Buckingham Gate. KING received substantial payment for his services, usually in sums varying from £50 to £200 at a time.

Early in 1936, PIECK was withdrawn from England, probably because he was thought to be under suspicion by the British authorities. Before

23

leaving, he handed KING over to his successor, "Mr. PETERSON", in reality Paul HARDT (q.v.), whom he introduced as the representative of a Dutch bank, thus keeping up the fiction that the whole operation was a purely financial racket. HARDT continued to control KING until June, 1937, when he told KING, that he had to leave England for a month or two. That, however, was the last KING ever saw of him and the end of KING's espionage activities.

KING was not exposed until just after the beginning of the war, when KRIVITSKY stated that the R.I.S. had an agent named KING in the Communications Department of the Foreign Office. This evidence pointed almost certainly to John Herbert KING, and by a curious coincidence it was confirmed within a few days by a statement volunteered by a Mr. Conrad PARLANTI. PARLANTI had been a partner of PIECK in the Buckingham Gate office, where PIECK had a room which he kept locked. PARLANTI eventually became suspicious of PIECK, discovered his photographic apparatus and extorted an admission from PIECK's wife that they were engaged in a big financial operation which involved access to Foreign Office documents. PIECK as good as admitted this to PARLANTI and offered to count him in but PARLANTI refused, and shortly afterwards broke off his business relations with PIECK. At one stage before this he had seen PIECK in company with a contact, whose description fitted KING, and PIECK had also once mentioned to him a "friend from the Foreign Office", who had been at a Brussels Conference, a fact which again pointed towards KING. PARLANTI, who had begun his association with PIECK in all innocence, had kept silent until September 1939, when he was apparently prompted by the outbreak of war to come clean.

King was arrested, tried, and sentenced to ten years' penal servitude in October, 1939. Helen WILKIE was discharged for a lack of evidence. KING was released in June, 1946, and is still living with Helen WILKIE.

Percy GLADING

The "Woolwich Arsenal Case", of which the leading figure was Percy GLADING, also forms part of the story of Paul HARDT and his network.

GLADING was born in 1893 and was employed on and off at the Royal Arsenal, Woolwich, for various periods. He was known as a prominent Communist from 1922 onwards and was also active in such organisations as the League against Imperialism[31]. As early as 1931 it was reported that all information about the Arsenal was to be passed to GLADING, who was engaged on special Communist Party work in that area, and also that he was the recipient of all military espionage reports from the United Kingdom intended for Moscow.

The network in the Arsenal was in fact a well-established one and had probably been in existence since the late twenties. The case did not break, however, till early in 1937, when it came to M.I.5. notice that GLADING was considering giving up his work as an open C.P.G.B. official and also his employment with the League against Imperialism. About the same time GLADING made an approach to a "Miss X", who had worked for a number of years for the League against Imperialism and the C.P.G.B., rising

24

to the position of secretary to Harry POLLITT.[32] Early in 1935 Miss X had resigned her job with the Party on (genuine) grounds of ill-health, but had kept in friendly touch with POLLITT and GLADING. The proposal which GLADING now made to Miss X was that he she should leave her home and become the nominal tenant of a flat to be used as a safe-house for secret meetings, photographic work, etc., and Miss X agreed to do this. GLADING was not to know that Miss X was in fact a long-term agent of M.I.5., who had patiently worked herself up, via the Friends of the Soviet Union and the League against Imperialism, to the key post of secretary and courier to Harry POLLITT himself.

A flat in Holland Park was duly rented and Miss X was visited there by GLADING, in company with his controller, who was introduced to Miss X as "Mr PETERS", but it is now known to have been Paul HARDT (q.v.). There was a good deal of talk about Miss X being required to photograph documents, but this did not materialise. Photography was however actually done at the flat by "Mr. & Mrs. STEVENS", later identified as Willy and Marie BRANDES, who succeeded Paul HARDT in control of the GLADING case after HARDT left England hurriedly in June, 1937. In October of that year Mrs. BRANDES was followed when she left the flat carrying a large parcel of plans which she had photographed in sections, and she was seen to hand the plans, wrapped in a roll of newspapers, to George WHOMACK, an employee of the Arsenal with known Communist sympathies, who took it home with him.

No arrests followed at this stage, and the BRANDES remained at liberty till they left for Moscow in November, 1937. GLADING was then left anxiously expecting the arrival of a new head of the network, since he was running very short of funds and he also did not know how to dispose of his material. One day towards the end of January, Miss X informed M.I.5. that GLADING had just left the flat to meet a man at Charing Cross form whom he was to receive material to be photographed. As a result, GLADING was watched and was seen to meet Albert WILLIAMS, an examiner of armaments at Woolwich, who handed to him a brown paper parcel. Both men were detained, and the parcel, when opened at Scotland Yard, was found to contain four blueprints. A search of GLADING's home revealed a store of photographic material, including plates of films containing military information.

GLADING was tried in March, 1938, together with George WHOMACK, Albert WILLIAMS and Charles MUNDAY, all Arsenal employees. MUNDAY was acquitted, but GLADING, WILLIAMS and WHOMACK, were sentenced to six, four and three years' penal servitude respectively.

It is not known how GLADING himself was recruited by the R.I.S but it is presumed that, using his previous associations with the Arsenal and its neighbourhood, he acted as talent-spotter among the employees there, as he had done for Miss X.[33] Although GLADING was to some extent the organiser of his own group of agents, he was always himself under control by Paul HARDT and then by Willy BRANDES, except for the period between BRANDES' departure and GLADING's arrest, during which GLAD-

ING was daily awaiting the arrival of a new controller. It is clear, however, that GLADING resented this foreign control and was planning to get the organisation into his own hands.

GLADING strangely enough, seems to have made no effort to provide himself with cover after giving up his Communist jobs. HARDT used the familiar GADA cover and BRANDES was nominally the agent for two American companies.

The plans and other documents were smuggled out of the Arsenal in the evening by GLADING's sub-agents there. They were then handed over to GLADING, immediately photographed, and returned to the sub-agent the same evening for replacement the following morning.

GLADING was released from prison in March, 1942, and in 1944 he resumed his full activities with the C.P.G.B. In 1946 there was a report that he still appeared to retain some authority over his former espionage agents. In 1951 he was said to be using the name Percy CLARK and to hold a very important position at King Street.[34]

WHOMACK was released from prison in June, 1940; in July, 1953, he was no longer regarded as a militant Communist. Williams was released in November, 1940. In 1950 he was known to be still a registered member of the C.P.G.B., and in the summer of that year he and his wife paid a holiday visit to Prague.

Wilfred MACARTNEY

No review of Russian espionage would be complete without a mention of Wilfred MCARTNEY, although his talent for mischief is by no means confined to the espionage field. He is indeed an Admirable Crichton of roguery and has committed (and been imprisoned for) almost every crime in the calendar, short of murder.

Born in 1898, MACARTNEY is a big, florid man, fond of drink and rich living. He is selfish quite unscrupulous and will do anything for money. He has lived (with varying success) on his wits since he dissipated his ample inheritance as a young man. He has a number of friends and acquaintances in high places (e.g. Aneurin BEVAN and Sir Compton MACKENZIE) over whom he claims to exert a powerful influence. The acquaintanceships are genuine, but his stories about them are suspect.

MACARTNEY's first conviction was in 1926, when he received nine months' imprisonment for breaking and entering a jeweller's shop. In April, 1927, he was charged with petty larceny, but the charge was later withdrawn. It is possible that MACARTNEY had to pay for the withdrawal of the charge by agreeing to work for the R.I.S.; at any rate about this time he was trying to obtain information about military aviation on a financial basis, from a certain George MONKLAND. MONKLAND having informed the authorities of this approach MACARTNEY, who was constantly travelling to and from the Continent, was kept under observation. He was eventually arrested in November, 1927, while keeping a rendezvous with a German agent of the G.R.U. named Georg HANSEN[35]. Both men were convicted of espionage on behalf of the U.S.S.R. and sentenced to ten years' penal servitude.

Released from prison in August, 1935, MACARTNEY continued to pursue his colourful way of life. Early in 1936 he is known to have met GLADING. Later that year he was recruiting for the Spanish Government forces; then after an interlude as a war correspondent and (most improbably) as dramatic critic, he commanded a battalion of the International Brigade. On his return to England, early in 1937, he published a book called "Walls Have Mouths", based on his experiences in prison. This turned out to be a best-seller, but the profits from it were evidently not enough to keep MACARTNEY for long in the state of life to which he was accustomed, since in March 1940 he was found guilty of obtaining credit by fraud from the Savoy Hotel and bound over for two years. In June, 1940 he was in contact with Douglas SPRINGHALL.

From 1940 to 1946 the record is a blank, but in the latter year MCARTNEY, with Eddie CHAPMAN[36], was fined for contravening the Official Secrets Act by helping to publish (in France) newspaper articles taken from CHAPMAN's book "Secret Service Convict". MACARTNEY then started to travel again very frequently and appears to have entered the arms traffic. In 1948 he was reported to have been negotiating for arms for the Jews in Palestine and also with the Russians in Stettin in connexion with the illegal sale of U.S. surplus equipment. In 1950 he was connected with an arms deal, allegedly for Haiti.

Meanwhile, he was in close contact with the C.P.G.B. and on intimate terms with leaders such as Harry POLLITT and George HORNER[37]. In 1949 he was said to be spreading Communist propaganda among Service personnel and also to be exploiting old contacts of SPRINGHALL in the industrial sphere. He is himself in turn exploited by POLLITT as a source of information, since; in addition to more reputable acquaintances already cited MACARTNEY is intimate with a wide variety of contacts, including a number of unsavoury businessmen and arms-traffickers.

There seems to be no guessing in what context this man of many parts will next choose to appear.[38]

Two minor pre-war cases.

Two minor cases from the pre-war period must be mentioned neither of which are connected with any of the big established networks.

Eric Joseph Camp @ GARDINER-CAMP, born in 1913, was a professed Communist. In 1936 he was convicted of obtaining plans from the Gloster Aircraft Company for Mikhail SOKOLOV[39], the Arcos representative in the United Kingdom, and was bound over for two years. In 1938 he was with the International Brigade in Spain. Camp was a poor creature, who was constantly in and out of prison and of various jobs, was once in a mental home and was also charged with bigamy. He was expelled from the C.P.G.B., but remained devoted to the cause.

Robinson WALKER was an engineer of some standing who was born in 1888. In July, 1938, while employed at Vickers Armstrong, he approached a fellow-employee named BURCH and asked him, for [text unreadable], to smuggle out certain plans. BURCH reported to the authorities and, acting under their instructions, handed the required plans to WALKER. WALKER was arrested with the plans on him, tried and sentenced to three year's penal servitude. He had been working under the control of Mikhail KAPTELSEV[40], an engineer serving with the Russian Trade Delegation, with whom WALKER had got into touch when he offered and invention to the Delegation. KAPTELSEV escaped conviction only by leaving the country as he heard of WALKER's arrest.

In 1942 WALKER applied for the post of Chief Technical Assistant at the Ministry of Supply. As Russia was by then in the war, he had no doubt hoped that bygones would be allowed to be bygones, but he was "not considered suitable".

Frederick MEREDITH & Wilfred VERNON.

When the Germans, in August, 1941, started a secret operation against an R.I.S. wireless station in Brussels, they gave the operation the code-name of "Rote Kapelle" ("Red Orchestra"). In course of time, however, this name has come to be applied to the GRU. Network – or more properly network of networks – in France, Belgium, Germany, Holland and Switzerland, which was eventually laid open by this operation. The story of the Rote Kapelle is a vast complicated one, with many ramifications, but for present purposes it is not necessary to summarise any of the component parts other that those which impinged more or less directly on the United Kingdom.

We need not deal at any length with the career of **Leopold TREPPER** a man of many aliases, although he was actually one of the greatest of the great line of pre-war-illegals. He does not seem, however, to have had any direct dealings with this country, even though from about 1934 onwards it formed part of his espionage empire, which also covered the Netherlands, France, Spain and Portugal. TREPPER continued to run a network in Paris and Brussels right through the earlier years of the war, until he was arrested by the Germans in December, 1942. He then talked freely, though he may have confined himself to facts which the Germans must already have known or were bound to discover. In any case, however, most of his group were arrested, including Henri ROBINSON (see below). TREPPER escaped from the Germans in September, 1943 and probably remained in hiding in France until nearly the end of the war. In January, 1945, he travelled in the same aircraft as FOOTE as far as Cairo, and was then on his way to Moscow under the alias Vladislav IVANOWSKI. His present whereabouts are unknown; he may still be in Moscow or again in the west. In 1948 there was a report the he was seen in Switzerland, but this could not be confirmed.[41]

We are more closely concerned with Henri ROBINSON, another of the great illegals, experienced, clever and versatile. ROBINSON was a man of many names and dubious origins, and even the date and place of his birth are uncertain. What is certain is that he became a Communist as a young man, and that by the middle twenties he was an important under-cover man for the Comintern. About 1930 he settled in Paris, and there first engaged in espionage for the G.R.U., starting with targets in Italy and France and later becoming responsible for a network of agents in the United Kingdom. Robinson travelled extensively during the pre-war period, and paid many visits (on a variety of passports) to Italy, Switzerland, Belgium, the United Kingdom, etc. He is an outstanding example of an illegal running a network in one country from a base in another. ROBINSON was relieved of the United Kingdom commitment after the fall of France, but continued to work against the Germans until his arrest at the end of 1942. He was however, clever enough even then to save a number of his agents, many of whom still remain unidentified. ROBINSON is believed to have been taken to Berlin for interrogation in 1943. According to one story he was then executed, but another report states that he was seen in the South of France in 1944.[42]

During the early thirties the head of the organisation in the United Kingdom was a very brilliant and polished agent known as HARRY I. By the time our period starts, however, he had disappeared for good from the English scene and had been succeeded by HARRY II, who was a very different type of man and almost theatrically foreign in appearance and manners. HARRY II, like ROBINSON, had his base in Paris and ran the United Kingdom network during 1936 and the first half of 1937. Among the agents for whom he is known to have been responsible during that period were Frederick William MEREDITH and Wilfred Foulston VERNON.

MEREDITH, who was born in 1895, was a very able research engineer working in the Royal Aircraft Establishment at Farnborough. He came to notice as a Communist in 1927 and in 1932 and 1935 he visited Russia. In 1935 he himself took the initiative by approaching Dorothy WOODMAN* and asking her to put him in touch with a Russian to whom he could pass information. Through her he was introduced to a Russian agent, afterwards identified as HARRY II, and by HARRY II to Ernst David WEISS (q.v. below). Through WEISS, Meredith passed secret information from R.A.E. first to HARRY II and later to Henri Robinson. In 1938 he resigned from the R.A.E. and is now employed with a firm engaged on classified Government work. He is no longer an open member of the C.P.G.B, but as late as 1951 was known to be to be expressing Communist and pro-Russian opinions.

*Dorothy WOODMAN, born in 1902, is a long-standing Communist who was probably recruited by the R.I.S as a talent-spotter during a visit to Russia in 1935. She wrote scholarly books and articles of some merit on the Far East &c. She contributes regularly to the "New Statesman" and also to the comforts of its editor, Kingsley MARTIN, whose mistress she is.

In 1948 MEREDITH admitted passing information to the Russians in the years from 1936, and said that he had done so because he was convinced that H.M.G. was sowing the seeds of disaster by its policy of hostility to Russia and acquiescence in German re-armament. On the basis of this interview an assessment was made of MEREDITH's character and probable re-actions in the event of a war against Russia, and as a result of this it was decided to allow him to remain on classified work, his technical brilliance being held to justify such a calculated risk.

Wilfred Foulston VERNON[43] was also an aircraft designer employed at Farnborough. He was active in the C.P.G.B. activities from about 1934 onwards and visited Russia twice, in 1935 and 1936. From 1936 onwards he was like MEREDITH, passing secret information through WEISS, first to HARRY II and later to Henri Robinson. He was probably present when MEREDITH was introduced to WEISS by HARRY II. In August, 1937, a burglary at VERNON's residence led to the discovery there of many secret documents. As a result VERNON was suspended from the R.A.E., charged under the Official Secrets Acts, and fined £50 – for the improper possession of these documents, it should be noted, and not for espionage, which was not at this stage suspected. His career, however, was by no means ended by this incident. In August, 1938, he was lecturing for the Left Book Club[44]; some time after December, 1939, he was in touch with a member of the Russian Embassy; and in 1940 he was a Home Guard Instructor (a favourite occupation also with many Left-wingers who had learned their guerrilla warfare with the International Brigade in Spain). In 1945, and again in 1950, VERNON was Labour M.P. for Dulwich, but he lost his seat in 1951. In 1952, he was in correspondence with MEREDITH, by whom he has (somewhat surprisingly) been described as a "most Christlike person".

When VERNON's espionage activities first became known, he was a Member of Parliament, and it was thought impracticable to prosecute him. He admitted, on interrogation, that he had been recruited by MEREDITH and had committed espionage, but he told little else.

Ernst David WEISS.

Ernst David WEISS, whose name has several times been mentioned, is of interest rather for his contacts and for the information he gave than for the actual work which he did, which was chiefly that of a cut-out. WEISS who was a German, born in 1902, combined the two somewhat heterogeneous professions of economist and one half of a two-piano act. He was recruited for the R.I.S. early in 1932 and in May of that year entered the United Kingdom with the nominal object of undertaking" industrial research". From then until February, 1934, he worked for HARRY I and from the autumn of 1935 to July, 1937, for HARRY II. In September, 1937, he met Henri ROBINSON in Jersey, and he saw ROBINSON for the last time in July, 1939. He thus forms a vital link in the chain HARRY I – HARRY II – ROBINSON. After 1939 (according to his own claim) WEISS's connexion with the R.I.S. ceased but it is possible that as late as 1941 he was in touch with ROBINSON's agent JEAN (see below), who was at that time stranded in England without funds.

WEISS became a naturalised British subject in 1946. In 1948 he was interrogated and admitted his espionage activities, implicating both VERNON and MEREDITH and giving important information about the two HARRY's and Henri Robinson. When last heard of, in 1953, he was living in London and working as a journalist. WEISS was in that year confronted with Ilse SAMUEL nee STEINFELD, who was the agent mistress of HARRY I and may also have worked for HARRY II, but the interview was unproductive.

Ilse Samuel is now married and living in a normal and comfortable way at Blackburn, but the love of her life was evidently HARRY I.

The "Robinson Papers".

It will be seen that up to 1937 at least there is ample evidence for the existence of a chain of "illegals" – Paul HARDT, PIECK, HARRY I, HARRY II Henri ROBINSON – all controlling agents in the United Kingdom though not necessarily residing here. It was, however, not until the end of the war that we learned positively of the existence of an illegal resident who was operating in the United Kingdom 1939 and 1940.

The evidence for this was supplied by the "Robinson Papers", the name usually given to a collection of letters and notes which were found by the Germans in ROBINSON's Paris house on his arrest in 1942 and were captured by the allies, along with other German intelligence records, in 1945 From these papers it appears that the illegal resident operating in the United Kingdom went under the name JEAN and was not properly registered here From the internal evidence of his letters it is clear that he was agent of the regular pre-war international type, who was equally at home in German French and English. JEAN has never been satisfactorily identified.

Among JEAN's agents in the United Kingdom (none of whom have been identified) were:-

• "Professor", a technician and electronics engineer. The only firm connexion between JEAN's network and any known individual is the fact that PROFESSOR had a friend called KALLMAN. KALLMAN is certainly identical with Heins Erwin KALLMAN, a German-American physicist, who probably acted as an unconscious source to PROFESSOR while he was in this country before March, 1939. PROFESSOR had a wife called SHEILLA.

• "BOB", whose value to the network would increase in war-time.

• "N", who lived in Liverpool and was the same age as BOB.

• A reliable friend of BOB.

An informant on the work of the Department of Overseas Trade.

• "M.P"'s friend". "M.P." was a French agent of ROBINSON's and is thought to be identical with Marcel PRENANT, a biologist and Communist leader. His "friend" is believed to be identical with a man described by AKHMEDOV[45] and referred to as "B". "B" was recruited by the Russian Intelligence Officer Maria POLAKOVA during her service in Western Europe and became a G.R.U. illegal resident in France. He escaped to the United Kingdom after Dunkirk and was instructed to obtain information on military targets in the Aberdeen area. Later "B" was on de Gaulle's staff. There was some talk of his making a place there for "M.P." but this was regarded as unnecessary when Moscow established a direct link with "B".

• "ADOLF", described as a Pole, who spoke French and German well was the contact of Franz SCHNEIDER, one of Henri ROBINSON's couriers when he visited London in 1938 and 1939. He is possibly identical with David WEISS.

• Apart from the DOCTOR and "B", AKHMEDOV spoke also of a G.R.U. female* agent in the United Kingdom, known as MARY, and of a girl or woman named ELLI. The unidentified ELLI lived in London in 1940 and is of considerable interest, since it has been alleged that she was in some way connected with the British intelligence services.

*It should be noted that an R.I.S. cover-name need not necessarily indicate the real sex of its bearer, though it does in this case.

The Rote Drei: FOOTE, RADO and the KUCZYNSKI family.

We need not go at any length into the history of the network known as Rote Drei, a subsidiary of the Rote Kapelle, which operated under Alexander RADO from bases in Switzerland during the years 1936 – 44. Working very much on its own (though with some links with Henri ROBINSON) this group was concerned solely with the German military, against which it scored remarkable successes. It was never engaged on espionage against the United Kingdom (it was indeed, in its own way, contributing to allied war effort), so that its only interest in the present context lies in the British origins and connexions of some of its members.

One of the British members was **Alexander Allan FOOTE**. FOOTE, who was born in 1906, was a man of the adventure type, uneducated but a good linguist. After a year in the R.A.F. he deserted and went as a volunteer to Spain, but in 1938 he was invalided back to England. It is believed that while in Spain he caught the eye of SPRINGHALL as a likely type; in any case, on his return he was approached by a Communist friend, Fred COPEMAN acting on behalf of SPRINGHALL, and asked to undertake a dangerous mission abroad. He agreed, and was sent by COPEMAN to a London flat where he met a woman (later identified as Brigitte LEWIS @ KUCZYNSKI – see below) who gave him instructions for a rendezvous in Geneva. There FOOTE met his contact, whom he then knew as "SONIA" and who was in fact Ursula KUCZYNSKI (@HAMBURGER @ BEURTON), the sister of his London contact Brigitte. After a period of training at Munich in wireless telegraphy &c, FOOTE was recalled to Switzerland, where he acted as chief wireless operator and general factotum for the RADO group until November 1943; when he was arrested by the Swiss police while actually transmitting. He was released on bail after ten months and made his way to Paris, where he contacted the Soviet Military Mission. From Paris he was flown via Cairo to Russia and there, after long interrogation, given an extensive course of training for a new mission which he was to undertake in the Argentine. On his way out through Berlin, however, FOOTE decided that he had had enough and went over with his story to the British authorities. He now writes newspaper articles as an expert on Russian espionage. His autobiographical "Handbook for Spies" is interesting and readable.

Alexander RADO, the head of the Rote Drei network, was a far from impressive personality, and the success of his organisation was largely due to one very remarkable source known as LUCIE[46], who had direct and rapid access to the secrets of all branches of the German armed forces. In September 1943 when one of his agents was arrested, RADO deserted the network and went into hiding. He eventually reached Paris and reported to the Soviet Embassy there. From Paris he was flown to Cairo on route for Russia, in the same aircraft which carried FOOTE and TREPPER. At Cairo, having a guilty conscience, he sought British protection, but this was refused and he completed the journey to Moscow. There was good reason to believe that he had been liquidated on arrival, since not only had he misappropriated R.I.S. funds, but there was also a suspicion that he had sold information to the British. It was therefore a matter of great surprise when in June, 1955, his wife Helene, who was living in Paris, received the first of a series of communications from her husband suggesting that he was still working for the R.I.S.

and due for another mission to the west. At the time of writing this, the matter has not yet been fully investigated; but if, as seems likely, RADO is really still alive and employed by the R.I.S., it raises interesting speculations about the real fate of some other agents who had been disgraced and presumed dead.[47]

The two KUCZYNSKI sisters, Brigette and Ursula, have been mentioned in connexion with FOOTE. Brigette (@ LEWIS @ LONG now NICOLSON) is an active long-standing Communist, but has not come to notice in an espionage context except in the FOOTE case. In addition to helping to recruit him she passed on messages to Moscow for him in 1941 when Moscow's wireless transmissions to Switzerland were interrupted.

Ursula, the older sister, is a more important figure. Born in Berlin in 1901, she was a Communist from her early days. Together with her husband Rudolf HAMBURGER, she worked in China for the R.I.S. from 1930 to 1935 and conducted a successful mission for them in Poland from 1936 to 1938. By the time she met FOOTE in October, 1938, she was established in Switzerland where she also met Leon BEURTON, a weak and ineffectual British recruit to her network. Having divorced HAMBURGER and married BEURTON, thus acquiring British nationality, she left Switzerland, on instructions from Moscow, in December, 1940, and made her way via Lisbon to England, which she reached in February, 1941. When interviewed by M.I.5 with her husband in 1947 she was completely un-cooperative and gave no information, but it is now known that in 1942/43 she was FUCHS' second contact, meeting him at regular intervals and receiving traffic for transmission to the Russians.

Ursula BEURTON was last heard of in East Germany in 1952.[48]

The third member of the enterprising KUCZYNSKI family known to have been engaged in espionage is Jurgen (@Peter FOERSTER, @ KARO), the elder brother of Brigitte and Ursula. A prominent member of the German Communist Party since about 1927, he was reported in 1939 to be involved in an O.G.P.U. espionage system in London. He was interned in January, 1940, but released in April as a result of pressure from influential quarters. Early in 1942, when FUCHS decided to pass information to the Russians, it was KUCZYNSKI who introduced him to Simon KREMER, the secretary to the Soviet Military Attaché in London. In the later part of the war, KUCZYNSKI served with the U.S. Air Force. In September, 1946 he became a lecturer at Berlin University and in September, 1949, Director of the German Institute of Economics in the Soviet Sector of Berlin. He was reported in 1950 to have been forced to resign from this post for deviationism, but to be still employed at Berlin University. In December 1955, he was in touch with headquarters of the C.P.G.B.[49]

Oliver Charles GREEN.

Oliver Charles GREEN was born in Birmingham in 1904; he was a printer by trade, and a diving instructor on the side. He first came to notice as a Communist in 1936 and early in 1937 he was in Spain, fighting with the International Brigade. On his return to England he moved from Birmingham to London, where he set up as a printer on his own, later becoming an A.R.P.

warden when his business fell off during the war.

In the middle of 1941 Scotland Yard discovered a case of forgery of petrol coupons and traced this to GREEN. He was arrested, and a search of his house revealed, among other things, two rolls of exposed films containing photographs of typed summaries derived from classified War Office papers. The police also found a small diary, the significance of which did not appear until later. GREEN was sentenced in February, 1942, to fifteen months' hard labour on the forgery charge. While in prison, he was interviewed by M.I.5, who had discovered from the films found in his house that he had been engaged in espionage. GREEN was induced to talk, but his statement was not complete, nor, it is believed, entirely accurate. As our knowledge of the case depends almost entirely on GREEN's own statement, plus the films and diary found in his house, there are inevitably gaps in the story.

According to GREEN's own account, which there is no reason to doubt on this point, he was recruited by a Russian while serving in Spain. He was immediately given some money and full instructions, in the approved R.I.S. style, for a rendezvous on his return to England. Early in 1938 he moved from Birmingham to London and set up his printing business as a cover for photographic work. He started his espionage activities, apparently with an entirely new network, early in 1939. GREEN's controller, who was also his first contact, in the United Kingdom, was a resident of the legal type. GREEN never knew his name, but it seems likely that he was an official of the Soviet Trade Delegation.

GREEN made little if any money out of his espionage, and his motives were entirely ideological, as apparently were those of most of his associates. He had fought in Spain because he was violently anti-fascist in his opinions, and his work for the R.I.S. was undertaken in the same spirit. GREEN had, however, out himself from the C.P.G.B. on his return from Spain, and for his agents he avoided using prominent members of the Party. These agents were placed in, or had access to, aircraft factories, the Merchant Navy and Government departments; they were widely scattered throughout the country, and it was the need for petrol to visit them by car which led to his downfall. All the usual conspiratorial techniques were used by GREEN and his agents at their meetings. The material received by GREEN from the agents was embodied by him in a typed report, which he then photographed twice. One film passed undeveloped to his controller and the other he kept until he learned that the first had reached its destination safely.

According to GREEN's own account, while working in this way to a 'legal' resident, he was also being groomed to act as an illegal resident himself in case of necessity. Such an emergency would have arisen, in the R.I.S. view, either if a fascist government had come into power and declared war on Russia or if the Germans had successfully invaded England. Either of these eventualities would have involved the closing of the Russian Embassy in London and thus the need for a stay-behind organisation to carry out espionage and sabotage against the new enemy. The sabotage side of the work would, according to GREEN, have been carried out by the C.P.G.B. under his instructions.

GREEN was released from prison in December, 1942. He continues to run his own printing and photographic business and remains a member of the Party. Not all of GREEN's known agents and associates have been identified. Among those whose names are known are:-

Joseph GARBER, who was probably recruited in Spain, and was thought by GREEN to be already running his own group in 1938. GARBER is still an ardent Communist, but has otherwise not come to security notice since the war.

Alan Ernest OSBORNE, the son of a naturalised German Jew whose original name was OETTINGER, had joined the Communist Party in 1938. His name was found among GREEN's papers, which showed that he had passed classified information to GREEN while serving in the army. OSBORNE who in 1935 was still a card-holding Communist, though somewhat shaken by the Slansky[50] trials in Prague, admitted in an interview with M.I.5 that he had worked for the Russians eleven years before, but told nothing about his associates.

Stanley George RAYNER, another member of the International Brigade was the chief wireless operator of GREEN's group and a timid nervous character. He later contracted T.B. and died in 1947.

Jack REID, (@ STEWART) was yet another veteran of the Spanish Civil War who is known, but only from delicate sources, to have belonged to GREEN's network. He is employed as a steward, sometimes on cross-channel boats, and his potentialities as a courier are obvious.

One of GREEN's more tantalising allusions was to somebody on "the security side" of the War Office who might inform the Russians of his defection if GREEN's name appeared in the reports on the M.I.5 interviews with him. GREEN had always understood that the R.I.S. possessed such a source of information, though he realised that the story might have been merely a bluff intended to boost his morale. This source (if one exists) has never been identified.

Douglas SPRINGHALL and his circle.

Consideration of the Rote Drei has led us imperceptibly past the crucial date – 22 June, 1941 – when Hitler invaded Russia. Up to this time to spy for Russia would have been, in the eyes of a patriotic Englishman, as foolish as it was criminal; after it, there were not lacking intelligent and conscientious people who regarded it as a positive duty to pass any available secret information into the hands of a great and gallant ally. It is always difficult to project the imagination backwards in time, even over twelve or fifteen years, but it cannot be too strongly emphasised that throughout the war period the life-and-death fight against Germany was exclusive pre-occupation of the average Englishman and woman. The Germans were, quite simply, the enemy and the Russians – albeit belatedly and in spite of their dubious past – the friends. Moreover, after June, 1941, the C.P.G.B. was supporting the anti fascist war, and at that period a known Communist in a position of trust in a Government department was no such anomaly as it has since become.

The case of Douglas Frank SPRINGHALL is of particular interest because of the high position which he occupied in the C.P.G.B. and hence of the Party's reaction to his exposure.

SPRINGHALL who was born in 1901, was a forceful and extrovert character, whose political views were never in any doubt. He was a foundation member of the C.P.G.B., and as early as 1920 he was discharged from the Royal Navy for Communist agitation. He rose steadily through the ranks of the Party, becoming a member of the Central Committee in 1932 and National Organiser in 1940. He visited Russia several times, and during the Spanish Civil War he held a political position with the International Brigade. At this time he probably noted as a talent-spotter (his nomination of FOOTE shortly afterwards is significant), but there is little evidence to show that he was engaged in any more active work for the R.I.S. before the war.

The story of SPRINGHALL's active espionage, as far as it is known, really starts in August, 1942, when under the alias PETER, he visited the flat of a Mrs. SHEEHAN, an Air Ministry employee and a left-wing sympathiser, whom he fascinated by an Othello-like account of his exciting earlier life. By this time Russia was in the war, and SPRINGHALL played on Mrs. SHEEHAN's sympathy with the Russians and on her indignation at the idea that we were withholding essential information from them. Early in 1943 Mrs. SHEEHAN was transferred to highly secret work, which she regularly discussed with SPRINGHALL. With almost unbelievable carelessness on SPRINGHALL's part, these conversations were carried on in Mrs. SHEEHAN's flat where they were overheard by her flat-mate Miss "A", a loyal citizen. In June, 1943, Mrs. SHEEHAN committed the further folly of entrusting Miss "A" with a letter for SPRINGHALL; this was steamed open by an R.A.F. officer in whom Miss "A" had confided and found to contain secret information about "window" and a list of left-wing sympathisers in the Air Ministry. This was damning evidence, and when PETER had been identified as SPRINGHALL he was sentenced, after a trial in camera, to seven years' imprisonment. Mrs. SHEEHAN got off with three months, but another associate, Ormond UREN, who was a serving officer, was cashiered and sentenced to seven years' penal servitude. Other contacts of SPRINGHALL were also known, but the evidence against them came from delicate sources and no prosecution was possible.

SPRINGHALL's conviction was very embarrassing for the C.P.G.B., which was taking great pains to appear respectable and was by then in favour of the war, and SPRINGHALL was expelled from the Party soon after his conviction. After his release in 1948 he was at first very bitter because the Party would have nothing to do with him, but they seem to have relented later, and in 1950 he visited China with a group of Party members who were going there to establish relations with the Chinese Communist Party. SPRINGHALL is believed to have died of cancer in Moscow in 1953.[51]

SPRINGHALL had no know R.I.S. contacts and it is not clear how far he was in control of a network on behalf of the Russians. His high position in the C.P.G.B. makes this, though possible, not very likely, and the ineptitude of SPRINGHALL's behaviour does not suggest the trained agent. Some of his work was certainly done on behalf of the Party for its own purpose, and all that can be said further with any certainty is that some at any rate of secret information which he acquired was passed to the Russians.

36

SPRINGHALL did not give evidence at the trial, and nothing is known about the channels by which his material was passed on.

Of SPRINGHALL's associates, Mrs. SHEEHAN was a left-wing sympathiser and a pro-Russian sentimentalist. It is not known precisely how SPRINGHALL first obtained her name. After her release from prison she obtained clerical employment and in 1948 was a full-time employee of the Civil Service Clerical Association and known to S.B. as a Communist or fellow-traveller.

Ormond Leyton UREN, born in 1919, was either a "closed member" of the C.P.G.B. or a sympathiser while he was at Edinburgh University just before the war. He joined the army as soon as war broke out and entered S.O.E. in May 1942. He was then becoming more outspoken in his Communist views, and in April, 1943, he was introduced to SPRINGHALL by Helen GRESSON, a Party member. Thereafter he handed over to SPRINGHALL a written description of the work of S.O.E., under the impression, as he claimed, that it was intended for the Central Committee of the C.P.G.B. Entries referring to UREN were found in SPRINGHALL's diary and, as has been said, UREN was sentenced to seven years' penal servitude. Through the intervention of D.N. PRITT, he was released from prison in December, 1947, before the expiry of his sentence. Prison, however, had not changed his views, and he remains a convinced Communist and a Party member. In 1952 he was deported from France as an undesirable alien. When last heard of, he was a master at a highly reputable preparatory school in London.

One of the luckier members of the SPRINGHALL circle was **Joseph Peter ASTBURY**. Born in 1916, he was a brilliant but erratic scientist who graduated from Cambridge in anthropology in 1938. While there he came to notice as a Communist. In 1943 he was serving with G.H.Q. Liaison Regiment and had invented a scrambling machine for high-grade cyphers. His name was found in SPRINGHALL's diary and he visited Communist Party headquarters on the day of SPRINGHALL's arrest. It was also known that he had met the Soviet Military Attaché in SPRINGHALL's company and had passed information to the Embassy, probably about signals equipment; but when interrogated ASTBURY bluffed it out, and the delicacy of the source of M.I.5's information about him saved him from prosecution.

ASTBURY has held various interesting scientific posts since the war including one under Professor BLACKETT in the Nuclear Physics department of Manchester University and one at the High Altitude Research Station on the Jungfraujoch. In 1954 he came back to England to take up a post in the physics department of the University of London.

He is known to have been in contact with Guy BURGESS.

Andrew ROTHSTEIN.

Another contact of SPRINGHALL's who also links up with several other interesting personalities, is Andrew ROTHSTEIN (@ ROEBUCK @ ANDREWS).

ROTHSTEIN, a British subject born of Russian parents in 1898, is a Communist and Soviet contact of very long standing. He is believed to have visited Russia as early as 1920, and by 1923 he was on the staff of the S.T.D. and a member of an organisation thought to be used as cover for Soviet espionage and the transmission of funds for subversive purposes. In 1926 he is said to have advised the N.K.V.D. to remove their secret documents from London because of the uncertainty of Anglo-Soviet relations. He was special correspondent of the newspaper "Trud" and made several secret trips abroad in Arcos ships. He was for a time on the Executive of the C.P.G.B. In 1934 he was in contact with FLOYD, who was then up at Oxford.

In 1935 ROTHSTEIN became a TASS correspondent, a post which he held in various places for many years. From 1936 to early 1939 he was in Geneva, where he was in contact with Helene RADO, wife of Alexander RADO of the "Rote Drei" network. Back in London, he was known in 1940 to be trying to obtain secret information about the R.A.F. from an agent. He was a friend of the Russian Ambassador MAISKY, and was believed to be working for the R.I.S. in 1942. In 1943, he was a known contact of SPRING-HALL and was described as the principal go-between for the C.P.G.B. and the Soviet Embassy. Later in 1943 ROTHSTEIN tool up work in the Russian section of the Ministry of Information under Harry SMOLKA (q.v.). In 1944 ROTHSTEIN was succeeded as head of TASS Agency in London by Vladimir ROGOV.

Since the war, ROTHSTEIN has been a Lecturer at the School of Slavonic Studies in London. He remains a leading member of the C.P.G.B., a prop of the U.S.S.R Friendship Society and a regular contact of the Soviet Embassy, acting as interpreter for visiting Russians.

Klaus FUCHS.

Klaus FUCHS was born in Germany in 1911, of a scholarly Quaker family. At Kiel University in 1932 he was already a keen anti-Nazi and a member of the Communist Party, and it was with the encouragement of the Party, which hoped for great things from FUCHS in the years to come that he left Germany in 1933 and came to the United Kingdom to complete his studies. FUCHS was a scholar and scientist of outstanding brilliance, and by 1939 he had taken his doctorate both at Bristol and at Edinburgh.

In May 1940, he was interned and sent to Canada.[52] Early in 1941, however, through the influence of a number of leading scientists, he was released and returned to the United Kingdom, to work first at Edinburgh University and then on the "Tube Alloys" (atomic energy) project at Birmingham. His work there was of sufficient importance to earn him naturalisation, a privilege which during the war was granted only in very exceptional cases, if deemed to be in the national interest.

As soon as he realised the significance of his work at Birmingham,

FUCHS decided to hand over information to the Russians, because he thought it would be "in the highest interests of humanity". It was his own view that he had recruited himself, but it seems possible that his mind had been prepared by Hans KAHLE, a well-known German Communist and suspected O.G.P.U. agent, with whom he had been intimate in his Canadian internment camp. Indeed, the first steps towards his recruitment may have been taken by the German Communist Party before FUCHS left Germany in 1933. Be this as it may, having decided to take action, FUCHS approached the German Communist, Jurgen KUCZYNSKI (q.v.), who put him in touch with Simon KREMER, the secretary to the Soviet Military Attaché in London. Between the end of 1941 and the end of 1942, FUCHS had at least four clandestine meetings with KREMER, and in 1943 the contact was taken over by a woman now known to have been Ursula BEURTON (q.v.) a sister of Jurgen KUCZYNSKI and an R.I.S. agent of long standing. At these meetings FUCHS handed over material which according to his own statement, consisted solely of spare copies of papers which he had written himself, and did not include the product of anybody else's brain.

In December, 1943, FUCHS was sent to the U.S.A. on the atomic energy project. Before going, he was briefed in detail by Ursula BEURTON about meeting a new contact in New York, with the full paraphernalia of recognition signals &c. The rendezvous was duly kept and FUCHS met the contact (now known to have been Harry GOLD[53]) several times during his stay in New York and handed over a substantial volume of information to him.

In August, 1944, FUCHS was transferred to Los Alamos to work on the atomic bomb, and from there he continued his meetings with GOLD .

Before FUCHS returned to England in June, 1946, to work at Harwell, GOLD gave him instructions for resuming contact with the R.I.S. in London. FUCHS, however, for his own reasons, did not keep this rendezvous and thus lost contact until early 1947. Having then decided to resume contact and failed to find Jurgen KUCZYNSKI, he sought the help of another German Communist and contact of KUCZYNSKI called Johanna KLOPSTECH. She agreed to help, and FUCHS duly met a new R.I.S. contact (never identified) in the usual conspiratorial manner in a north London pub, only to be rated for establishing contact through the Communist Party (FUCHS took this to imply that KLOPSTECH had arranged matters for him through the C.P.G.B.). Nevertheless, a series of further meetings with the same contact took place over the next two years in the usual circumstances of secrecy. Gradually, however FUCHS became less enthusiastic about his espionage activities and started to question the actions of the Russians and C.P.G.B. He accordingly began to taper off the amount of information he was passing and eventually, after missing one meeting through illness, he deliberately failed to take up the thread again. So far is known, the Russians made no attempt to restore the contact.

In August, 1949, it became known that there had been a serious leakage to the Russians of atomic information, which could only have come from a British scientist working in the U.S.A. in 1944.[54] The possible sources were narrowed down to FUCHS alone, and eventually, after a series of interviews with M.I.5. he made a full confession of his espionage activities. FUCHS was arrested in February 1950 and received the maximum sentence, i.e. fourteen years' imprisonment. In subsequent interviews he has identified only four of his contacts – KUCZYNSKI, KREMER, GOLD and KLOPSTECH.

There is no doubt that FUCHS is one of the clearest examples of the purely ideological spy and that he was motivated solely by cloudy notions about the good of humanity. It is significant that he never received any money from the R.I.S. beyond his expenses until after he returned to the United Kingdom in 1946, when he accepted a payment of £100. This, in his own words, was to be regarded as a symbolic payment signifying his subservience to the cause.[55]

Alan NUNN MAY.

The case of Alan NUNN MAY does not strictly belong to this paper, since his keen espionage activities were confined to Canada. It would, however, seem to be pedantic to exclude so notorious a figure on a pure technicality.

NUNN MAY, who was born in Birmingham in 1911, was at Trinity Hall, Cambridge, from 1930 to 1936, a vintage period for Communist and R.I.S. recruits. He was an ardent but secret Communist from early days and is said to have been known to, if not recruited by, the R.I.S. for a number of years before he became active in espionage.

NUNN MAY, as a scientist and a war-time civil servant, went to Canada in 1943 to work under Cockcroft as a group-leader on the atomic energy project, a post which gave him access to substantial information about the whole programme. He was left alone by the Russians for some time, but at the end of 1944, on instructions from Moscow, he was contacted by Pavel ANGELOV[56], who worked in the office of Colonel ZABOTIN[57], the Military Attaché and G.R.U. Resident. Through this channel NUNN MAY passed over small samples of uranium and information on the first atomic bomb. He also provided information about other subjects, such as the proximity of fuses used for anti-aircraft shells.

When NUNN MAY was about to return to England in September 1945, detailed arrangements were worked out by ZABOTIN for him to make a new contact in London, with the usual paraphernalia of recognition signals and passwords – arrangements which Moscow, with typical fussiness, then proceeded to alter in every respect. NUNN MAY, however, did not keep the rendezvous since, according to his own later statement, he had by then decided "that this clandestine procedure was no longer appropriate in view of the official release of information and the possibility of satisfactory international control of atomic energy". He claimed not to have acted from mercenary motives, but he did in fact receive payment for his work.

The defection of GOUZENKO[58] led to the exposure of NUNN MAY, who was convicted and sentenced to ten years' penal servitude. He was released in December, 1952, since when he has found scientific employment at Cambridge. His political views remain unchanged, and in August, 1953 he married Dr. Hildegarde BRODA, a Communist and the former wife of Engelbert BRODA, who may have recruited NUNN MAY for the R.I.S., though proof of this is lacking.[59]

David FLOYD and Arthur WYNN

David FLOYD, born in 1914, was an active Communist from his youth, and as early as 1933 he served a prison sentence for creating a disturbance in a cinema. While up at Oxford he was a secretary for the October Club[60] and organiser of the Oxford branch of the Communist Party.

On coming down from Oxford he went through a strange variety of occupations, being in turn an employee of John Lewis & Co., secretary of the Listeners League, a milk roundsman and a Probation Officer. In 1939 he married Joan DABBS, a Communist whom he had known at Oxford. In 1941 he joined the R.A.F. and, after a course at the School of Slavonic Studies, was commissioned in the Intelligence Branch and posted to the British Military Mission in Moscow early 1944.

The story of FLOYD's espionage activities is based on his own subsequent statement to M.I.5. According to this, before leaving for Russia, FLOYD had approached his old friend Arthur WYNN (see below) and asked that the Soviet authorities might be informed of his posting to Moscow. FLOYD then had a clandestine meeting with a R.I.S. agent in London and received instructions in familiar R.I.S. style, for making contact in Moscow. In May, 1944, this contact duly took place, and FLOYD met his permanent R.I.S. "friend", whom he knew as Victor Nikolaievich. FLOYD was transferred to the Foreign Office staff at the British Embassy late in 1945, having meanwhile been in frequent contact with the R.I.S. either through Victor or through and anonymous woman language-teacher. In the spring of 1946, FLOYD met a Russian girl Liddia Mikailovna MARIENBACH, who was almost certainly working for the R.I.S., and who became his mistress. Her flat was regularly used for meetings with Victor, whose chief interest was in obtaining information about the British Embassy staff and in British agents and sources in Russia.

In 1946, FLOYD's wife divorced him, citing Liddia as co-respondent. Having been posted to Prague, FLOYD then married not Liddia but a Czech women, which necessitated his being posted away from there, this time to Belgrade. Here he again met Victor and was also in contact with SHNIVKOV, the Soviet Charge d'Affairs, and with Vladimir KARMANOV[61], an R.I.S. agent.

In 1950, at the instance of the Foreign Office, M.I.5 carried out a check on FLOYD. In July, 1951, while he was in England, he made a voluntary confession of the activities summarised above, but the Director of Public Prosecutions advised against legal action.

FLOYD is now on the staff of the "Daily Telegraph" and (not surprisingly) is recognised as its Russian expert.

Arthur WYNN is a long-standing Communist and the husband (successively) of two Communist wives, who was a friend of FLOYD and his political mentor at Oxford. In 1939 he and his wife were witnesses at FLOYD's first wedding. When interviewed in July, 1951, soon after FLOYD's confession, WYNN flatly denied having been implicated in FLOYD's introduction to the

R.I.S. Since therefore it is simply a case of one man's word against another's, it is impossible to say with certainty which of the two is lying. On the other hand, while there seems to be no obvious reason for FLOYD to have invented the story, there is every good reason for WYNN to deny it.

WYNN is a man of great ability, who has worked his way, via the Ministry of Fuel and Power, to the position of full-time member of the National Coal Board. Before FLOYD's confession he had been through the purge procedure[62] and had successfully passed the ordeal of the "Three Wise Men", [63] it being then believed that he had lived down his Communist past. Subsequent events, however, have revived the interest of the Security Service in him.

BURGESS and MACLEAN

It is difficult to know exactly where to place BURGESS, MACLEAN and their associates, since their espionage activities extended from right back in the pre-war days, through the shotgun wedding and the honeymoon period with Russia, into the black days of the cold war.

So many oceans of ink have been spilled over the case that it does not seem profitable, or even practicable, to include any short summary of it here. Instead, there is appended a skeleton chronology of the lives of BURGESS and MACLEAN, in parallel columns, which shows where each of them was and how they were employed at any given time.

Some of their contacts, who have not come so much into the public eye are treated rather more fully below.

BURGESS.

- 1911 16 April, BURGESS born.

- 1930-33 At Trinity Hall, Cambridge, Communist.

- 1934-35 Research Work and teaching at Trinity.

- 1935 Probably left the C.P.G.B.

- 1936 Joined the B.B.C.

- 1937 Probably started espionage activities; continued them throughout.

- 1938 Outside agent for S.I.S.

- 1939 January. Joined S.O.E.

- 1940 September. Left S.O.E.

- 1941 January. Re-joined B.B.C. Worked as outside agent for M.I.5.

- 1944 Joined the Foreign Office (News Department) as temporary officer.

- 1946 Ceased to work for M.I.5. December P.A. to Hector McNeill as

Minister of State.

- 1947 January. Established in the Foreign Office.
- 1950 August. Second Secretary, British Embassy, Washington.
- 1951 1 May. Left U.S.A, on recall to U.K. 7 May Arrived in U.K.

MACLEAN.

- 1913 25 May, MACLEAN born.
- 1931-34 At Trinity Hall, Cambridge. Communist.
- 1935 October. Left the C.P.G.B. Joined the Foreign Office
- 1936-37 Believed to be KRIVITSKY's "Imperial Council Source" continued espionage activities throughout.
- 1938 September. Posted to Paris.
- 1940 May. Married Melinda MARLING in Paris.
- June Escaped to England before German invasion.
- 1944 May. Posted to Washington.
- 1948 November. Counsellor, British Embassy, Cairo.
- 1950 May. Returned to England on sick leave.
- November. Head of the American Department, Foreign Office.

1951, 25 May BURGESS and MACLEAN left England.

1953 September Mrs. MACLEAN and children disappeared from Switzerland.

1955, September PETROV's revelations and the U.K. Government White Paper published.

1956, 11 February BURGESS and MACLEAN held a Press Conference in Moscow.

John CAIRNCROSS

It will be seen that the paths of BURGESS and MACLEAN hardly crossed between their Cambridge days and their flight to Russia, so that it is not correct to think in terms of a "BURGESS-MACLEAN circle". Each of the two, however, independently left a trail of contacts of intelligence interest, which in some cases were duplicated. These contacts were for the most part men of exceptional intellect, enjoying a position in the world which gave them access to classified political information of high importance. The known facts about some of these contacts must therefore now be summarised.

John CAIRNCROSS is a Scot, born in 1913, who had a fine academic record at Glasgow University and Trinity College, Cambridge, where he was also an enthusiastic member of the C.P.GB. At this time, BURGESS was still up at Trinity doing post-graduate research, and CAIRNCROSS certainly met him early in 1937, if

43

not before. In 1936, CAIRNCROSS had entered the Foreign Office as a Third Secretary, and in 1937 he was serving in the Spanish Section with MACLEAN. He was, however, regarded by the Foreign Office as not being the diplomatic type, and in October, 1938, he was transferred to the Treasury. Early in 1939 he arranged the entry into the United Kingdom of Victor HAEFNER[64], a former international spy, through whom he became implicated in the arms traffic to Spain and Greece. A little later he was collecting information on British foreign policy from well-placed Government sources and passing it to BURGESS. In 1939 and 1940, during his frequent trips to Paris, he again met MACLEAN, who as en poste there. He was employed for a year at G.C.H.Q. in 1942/43 and in S.I.S from 1943 to 1945, after which he returned to the Treasury. In May, 1951, he was again transferred, this time to the Ministry of Supply, but in December he reverted to the Treasury.

After MACLEAN's flight, CAIRNCROSS's name and telephone number were found in his diary against a date about five weeks earlier. CAIRNCROSS was twice interviewed by M.I.5 after the disappearance of BURGESS and MACLEAN, and was shaken but unhelpful. When interviewed a third time in March, 1952, he at first denied any close contact with BURGESS, but later admitted the authorship of a fifteen-page intelligence report which had been found among BURGESS's possessions. Two days later, having in the meanwhile consulted a shady firm of solicitors and used what might well have been a D.L.B. in Hyde Park, he made a formal statement pleading that youthful indiscretion and a desire to ingratiate himself had led him to supply the information asked for by BURGESS.

A few days later, CAIRNCROSS was observed travelling to a rendezvous with an unknown person and using characteristic R.I.S. evasion techniques. When interviewed again and questioned about this incident, he gave a most unlikely explanation. Next day, however, he voluntarily admitted that this was a complete fabrication and told a new entirely different story, which could in no way be checked but which represented his recent rendezvous as a date with a mysterious Frenchwoman.

Two days later CAIRNCROSS's resignation from the Civil Service was accepted. Since then he has lived in Rome, first as a part-time representative of "The Observer" and later as a correspondent of the Canadian Broadcasting Corporation. At yet another interview with M.I.5 in August, 1954, he was again uncommunicative.

The Communist thread appears at intervals throughout his career.[6566]

NORMAN KLUGMAN

Norman James KLUGMAN, an English Jew, was educated at Gresham's School, Holt, where he was already reported to have had a Communist influence over his contemporaries, among them being MACLEAN, his junior by a year. In 1930 KLUGMAN went up to Trinity, Cambridge, where he was an intimate friend of BURGESS, whom he may have introduced to the Russians.[67] He also continued to exert a considerable influence over MACLEAN, who had gone up to Trinity Hall in 1931. He is said to have been secretary of the University Communist cell and to have advised prospective members of the Diplomatic Service to let their Communist Party membership lapse and go underground.

KLUGMAN, who is a fine linguist,[68] continued doing research at Trinity (as did BURGESS) in 1934 and 1935. From the latter year he is known to have been engaged in espionage for the Comintern, under whose orders he was working. In 1939, in agreement with the Comintern, he tried (unsuccessfully) to enter the Intelligence Service. He was called up as a private in the R.A.S.C. late in 1940 and it was not till February, 1942, that he joined S.O.E. where he became a specialist on Yugoslavia. It is now known, from a very delicate but reliable source, that from 1942 onwards KLUGMAN used his position as a controller and despatcher of agents into Yugoslavia to favour the (pro-Russian) Partisan forces as against the Chetniks, who were at that time supported by H.M.G, by ensuring that only reports favourable to the Partisans filtered through to higher authority.

From April, 1945, KLUGMAN was in Belgrade as assistant to the head of the U.N.R.R.A. mission to Yugoslavia, a Russian, to whom he passed information. He was then approached by an R.I.S. agent, who knew his past history pressed him to work for the R.I.S. again. KLUGMAN was reluctant to jeopardise the organisation which he had built up in Yugoslavia, but eventually he agreed and some unimportant traffic passed.

There is no doubt that, in spite of his denials when questioned KLUGMAN has always been a faithful active Communist. Since the end of the war he has continued to be an official of the C.P.G.B. and has been prominent in its educational activities. He has also been in contact with the Press Department of the Russian Embassy and with a number of Satellite diplomats.[69]

Harry SMOLKA

Harry Peter SMOLKA (@ SMOLLETT) is an Austrian Jew, born in Vienna in 1912 and a man of great intellectual brilliance. His first espionage trace occurs as a early as 1930, when he photographed a French fort and was arrested and expelled from France as an Italian spy. From then onwards his home was in the United Kingdom, where he was naturalised in 1938. His frequent visits abroad, which were proper to his journalistic business, included two trips to Russia.

In 1939 SMOLKA (who had officially changed his name to SMOLLETT on his naturalisation) was in Switzerland and Roumania on business, with Foreign Office letters of introduction, and it was on the recommendation of the Foreign Office that in September, 1939, he was appointed to the News Department of the Ministry of Information, from which, shortly afterwards a leakage of information to Switzerland was suspected. Early in 1940 SMOLKA was involved in an incident in which two central European refugees were found operating a large wireless receiver in his Hampstead house. In July 1940, SMOLKA applied, without success, for employment in Military Intelligence, and in December, 1941, he was transferred to the Soviet Relations Branch of the Ministry. In this capacity he attempted through his contacts, to place a Communist friend as S.I.S. representative in Russia, and it is now known that from October, 1941, to May, 1942, he was compiling and passing to BURGESS information of a secret character. Before resigning from the Ministry in 1945, SMOLKA was rewarded for his services with the O.B.E.

Since the war, SMOLKA has worked in Czechoslovakia and Vienna as a correspondent for the "Daily Express" and the "Times". In March, 1953, he was living and working in the Soviet Zone of Vienna, and was described as a "dyed-in-the-wool" Communist. SMOLKA has suffered severely from diabetes and may not be a good life.[70]

William Martin Marshall

It will be realised that, though the activities of BURGESS and MACLEAN covered many years, their detection took place after the development of the cold war and the worsening of Anglo-Russian relations, which at the time of Korea might well have passed into a shooting war. There have, however, been few detected cases of Russian espionage in this country which are known to have actually developed during that period. For this there are many possible reasons – the intensified security measures in Government offices and in factories engaged in classified work, including the purge procedure; the increased public awareness of the threat and a natural reluctance to work for the Russians, as contrasted with the feelings of good will towards them during the war-time honeymoon period; the bad luck – or perhaps dimin-

45

ished efficiency – of the Security Service. The real cause is probably a mixture of all these factors. One encouraging feature, however, is the number of approaches which are now reported at an early stage, leading in many cases to useful D/A operations and this to an improved knowledge of R.I.S. personalities and techniques.

It remains therefore to summarise one or two isolated cases which have emerged in recent years, but which have no discoverable connexion with any other network.

The first is that of William Martin MARSHALL, a young wireless operator who, after leaving the army, joined the Diplomatic Wireless Service in November, 1948. In December, 1950, he was posted as a matter of administrative convenience to Moscow, a posting which was known also to be in accordance with his own wishes. He was, however, a misfit in Moscow, where the conditions were admittedly difficult, and his work deteriorated to the point where his transfer was considered. He was nevertheless allowed to complete his tour and he returned to England in December 1951, not before he had caused considerable concern by disappearing from the Embassy for the better part of the day on which he was due to leave Moscow.

On his return to England MARSHALL took up duty at the D.W.S. station in Buckinghamshire. In April, 1954, while on leave from this station, he was observed at Kingston in the company of Pavel KUZNETSOV, Second Secretary at the Soviet Embassy. While they were together, MARSHALL was seen to produce papers from his pocket and to show them to KUZNETSOV, who made notes about them. One other meeting between MARSHALL and KUZNETSOV was observed before 13 June, on which date they were apprehended by the police in St. George's Park, Wandsworth. On identifying himself as a diplomat, KUZNETSOV was released, but after MARSHALL's trial he was withdrawn from the United Kingdom at the request of the Foreign Office.

When Marshall was arrested, he was found to be carrying a wallet containing details of the call-signs, frequencies, etc., of the Diplomatic Wireless service in his own handwriting. His diary also showed that he had met KUZNETSOV six times before they were first observed together. At his trial MARSHALL was found guilty on four charges under the Official Secrets Acts and sentenced to five years' imprisonment. After failing in an appeal, he duly served his sentence, and was released in December, 1955 having earned full remission for good conduct.

MARSHALL's motives for espionage and the method of his recruitment are still not entirely clear. It appears likely, however, that he had begun to be interested in Communism and to take the "Daily Worker" in 1948. While in Moscow he was impressed by the efforts and ideals of the Russian people. Being of an introspective and unsociable nature he did not fit easily into the very restricted British society available to him in Moscow, and he found his outlet in regular visits to Russian cinemas. His character and circumstances must have made him easy meat for the R.I.S., and it is possible that his recruitment was effected through one of the Russian women in the domestic staff of the Embassy.

Ajit Kumar GUPTA

A small boy is the hero of the next story. While walking in Canon's Park, Edgware, in March, 1954, he noticed a loose brick in a wall. On removing it, he found in the hole behind it a brown paper packet, which he took home. It was opened by his parents, who found inside it four hundred English pound notes and an unsigned typewritten letter, which they duly reported to the police. The police kept the site of the find under observation, and on the same evening an Indian, Ajit Kumar GUPTA, was seen to approach and loiter in the area. Next afternoon a Russian appeared and examined the hiding place; he was later identified as Andrei Fedorovich

GUDKOV, an Assistant Military Attaché.

Gupta made a statement to the police and appears to have concealed little of his story. Born in 1918, he became a card-holding member of the Indian Communist Party in 1942 and next year a full-time paid official of the Party. He resigned in 1948 as a result of a split in the Party, but remained a convinced Marxist, and attended a number of shows sponsored by the Soviet Embassy in Delhi. Here he met an unidentified Russian, to whom he confided his earlier membership of the Communist Party.

In July, 1953, GUPTA was proposing to sell up the small business which he had established and go to Switzerland for medical treatment. His Russian friend then offered to arrange some business introductions for him in Switzerland, and gave him instructions for making a contact in Berne. These instructions were purely conspiratorial, in the approved R.I.S. style, but they did not (at least according to his own story) rouse any suspicions in GUPTA's mind.

GUPTA duly made contact in Berne with an unidentified man who spoke English but was not an Englishman. Instead of arranging any business introductions in Berne, however, this man suggested that GUPTA should go on to England, where introductions into business circles would be arranged. GUPTA was given the large sum of about £1,000 in Swiss notes for his expenses and received elaborate instructions for making further contact in London, complete with recognition signals, passwords and alternative rendezvous.

On arriving in London, GUPTA duly left a cigarette packet at the prescribed place and at the second attempt achieved a meeting in Acton with a Russian, later identified as GUDKOV. GUDKOV made it clear that GUPTA was intended to provide information from the Indian High Commissioner's office in London, at any rate for a start. When GUPTA jibbed at this and talked of introductions which he had been promised, GUDKOV replied – not without reason – that GUPTA should have guessed the kind of business for which it was proposed to use him. GUPTA (according to his own story) repeated his refusal to engage in espionage and asked for passages back to India for himself and his family. GUDKOV answered that he would have to consult his superiors, and arranged a further series of signals, one of which was to indicate whether any expenses which he might claim would be allowed or whether there was any other message for him. On receiving such signal, GUPTA went to the d.l.b at Canon's Park, with the results which have been described.

GUPTA denied that he had ever supplied the Russians with any information and claimed – somewhat unconvincingly – that he had travelled to Switzerland and then on to England in all good faith and in the expectation of business advantage. His case was not considered suitable for a prosecution and he was allowed to return to India, the Indian authorities being kept fully informed. GUDKOV was declared persona non grata and left England, not however before he had made a last-minute attempt to buy information from the Finnish Military Attaché.

The GUPTA case, though of very minor importance in itself, is interesting as showing the amount of money and trouble which the R.I.S. were willing to expand on such a target as the Indian High Commissioner's Office in London, and also as illustrating a most elaborate form of technique in arranging meetings and passing messages.

Tailpeace - John CLARENCE

The last story in this series forms an epilogue with a strong note of low comedy.

John CLARENCE, born in 1927, elected to serve another three years in the

47

army after his national service ended late in 1948. He had joined the Young Communist League in 1943, but first came to security notice in 1946 as an alleged sympathiser with Nazism. On being convicted for larceny and forgery in 1946, CLARENCE had asked for twenty-two similar cases of forgery to be taken into consideration. He was stated to have "taken fits" in his early years.

In October, 1951, while on leave from the army CLARENCE was found wandering about France dressed in an officer's uniform of his own design and describing himself as the Duke of Clarence, engaged on a special mission. He was brought home and diagnosed as schizophrenic, but was discharged from hospital in January, 1952.

In March, 1952, having left the army, he joined the C.P.G.B. and soon became Treasurer of his local branch. In September, however, he was suspended from the Party, and later formally expelled, for pocketing Party funds using the Party as cover for homosexual approaches.

About this time CLARENCE, whose Communist ardour had not been damped by his expulsion, approached the Soviet Embassy and probably received some sort of commission from Ivan Ilyich BARABANOV,[71] a Second Secretary and a known Intelligence officer to work for the Embassy in the émigré field and to distribute propaganda, for which he received small payments at odd times. There is, however, reason to believe that the C.P.G.B. had warned the Embassy of CLARENCE's unreliability, and his "commission" from BARABANOV may well have been one of many flights of imagination.

In November, 1952, CLARENCE called at U.S. naval headquarters in London (in the middle of the night) and offered to provide British information to the Americans. He supported his claim to notice by typing out then and there what purported to be his monthly report to BARABANOV; this was later found to be a tissue of nonsense.

In August, 1953, CLARENCE got a post as a civilian clerk with an anti-aircraft battery in Northumberland. He was not vetted until October, when he was dismissed on the strength of his past history. His departure coincided with the burning out of the battery headquarters, CLARENCE being the last to leave the building.

CLARENCE then came south again, leaving behind him a trail of dud cheques. Back in London, after further acts of fraud and a period of posing as "Agent of the German Democratic Republic", he hired a book stall in a public market in south-east London. Here he was indiscreet enough to leave behind him a despatch-case which, on being opened by the police, was found to contain a note, with the pencilled heading "Embassy – Soviet Union", describing accurately the organisation of the anti-aircraft defences in the Tyne area.

Clarence (who was already in prison for one of his frauds) was prosecuted under the Official Secrets Acts. He insisted on conducting his own defence and was sentenced to another five years' imprisonment.

It will be noted that there was nothing to show that the R.I.S. had solicited CLARENCE's information about anti-aircraft defences and that BARBANOV's only involvement – in that a problematical one – was with his earlier EM activities. The Foreign Office accepted the Soviet Embassy's explanation, and BARABANOV was not removed.

The comment of King Street on the case was that the Foreign Office must have been "been hard pressed" to bother about CLARENCE at all. Maybe in this case King Street was not so far wrong.

FIGURE 1: FACISM: BENIT MUSSOLINI AND ADOLF HITLER "BERLIN-ROME PACT" 29.9.1938

FIGURE 2: MOLOTOV'S VISIT TO THE UNITED KINGDOM TO SIGN THE 20 YEAR MUTUAL AID PACT 1942.

FIGURE 3: THEODORE MALY AKA PAUL HARDT . CODENAME "MANN", "PAUL" & "THEO"

FIGURE 4: HEDE MASSING - ACTRESS - NKVD AGENT CODENAME "REDHEAD"

FIGURE 5: EDITH TUDOR-HART, NEE SUSCHITZKY, CIRCA 1936. "EXPERT PHOTOGRAPHER".

Alexander Allan FOOTE   Alexander RADO   Brigette KUCZYNSKI

Leon BEURTON   Rudolph HAMBURGER   Ursula KUCZYNSKI

FIGURE 6: FOOTE, RADO AND THE KUCYZYNSKI"S

FIGURE 7: GEORGE WHOMACK A SIB-AGENT FOR PERCY GLADING

FIGURE 8: WILFRED MCCARTNEY

FIGURE 9: WILFRED FOULSTON VERNON

FIGURE 10: ERNST DAVID WEISS

FIGURE 11: ATOMIC SPY KLAUS FUCHS IS MET BY HIS NEPHEW HLAUS KITTOWSKI AT SCHOENFELD AIRPORT AFTER BEING RLEASE FROM PRISON WHERE HE SERVED 9 YEARS AND 3 MONTHS OUT OF A 14 YEAR SENTENCE. CODENAME "CHARLES, "REST".

FIGURE 12: ALAN NUNN MAY. "CODENAME ALEK"

FIGURE 13: GUY FRANCIS DE MONCY BURGESS. CODENAME "MADCHEN".

FIGURE 14: DONALD DUART MACLEAN. CODENAME "ORPHAN"& "HOMER".

FIGURE 15: MELINDA MACLEAN NEE MARLING. SEPTEMBER 1953, MRS MACLEAN AND CHILDREN DISAPPEARED FROM SWITZERLAND.

FIGURE 16: JOHN CAIRNCROSS. CODENAME "LISZT" & "MOLIÈRE"

FIGURE 17: NORMAN KLUGMAN. CODENAME "MER"

FIGURE 18: HARRY (PETER) SMOLKA. CODENAME "ABO"

FIGURE 19: WILLIAM MARTIN MARSHALL

FIGURE 20: THE ITALIAN NATIONAL COMMUNIST CONGRESS 1948: HARRY POLLITT GENERAL SECRETARY OF THE COMMUNIST PARTY OF GREAT BRITAIN (1929-1956) WITH PALMIRO TOGLIATTI HEAD OF ITALY'S COMMUNIST PARTY AND MAURICE THOREZ FRENCH COMMUNIST LEADER.

FIGURE 21: LEOPOLD TREPPER "A MAN OF MANY ALIASES" PHOTO TAKEN IN 1973 WHEN HE ARRIVED IN THE UK TO BE TREATED FOR A BLOOD DISEASE ORDER AT ST THOMAS' HOSPITAL LONDON.

FIGURE 22: WALTER GERMANOVICH KRIVITSKY DEFECTED TO THE WEST IN OCTOBER 1937. HE WAS FOUND DEAD IN HIS HOTEL ROOM IN WASHINGTON 10 FEB 1941 WITH A GUNSHOT WOUND TO THE RIGHT TEMPLE.

Chronological Table

In the original MI5 chronological table it was split into two parts General and R.I.S. In the below table bold text represents the **General** events and plain text represents the R.I.S. (Russian Intelligence Service) events.

1935

March	***The Saar returned to Germany.***
	Hitler denounces disarmament clauses of Versailles.
	Leopold TREPPER head of GRU W. Europe and U.K.
Early	J.H. KING started passing F.O. Information to PIECK (active in U.K. and W. Europe, 1932 – 1936)
	Norman KLUGMAN started espionage
June	Paul HARDT chief OGPU agent in U.K.
August	Wilfred MACARTNEY released after serving ten years sentence for espionage.
September	KRIVITSKY head of GRU in W. Europe.
October	***Italy invaded Abyssinia***
	Donald MACLEAN joined the Foreign Office.
Autumn	HARRY II succeeded HARRY I as head of OGPU network in U.K. Living in Paris.

1936

March	**Hitler remilitarised the Rhineland in defiance of Versailles and Locarno.**
	O.C. GREEN came to notice as M.C.P.
	Wilfred VERNON started to pass R.A.E. information to the Russians
	MACLEAN probably started working for the R.I.S.

68

Spring	Frederick MEREDITH started to pass information from R.A.E. to the Russians.
July	*Spanish Civil War started.*
June	Paul HARDT left England finally and went to Russians
August	*Trial and execution of the first party of "Old Bolsheviks" in Moscow.*
Autumn	*"Berlin-Rome" Axis.*
October	Eric CAMP convicted and bound over for obtaining Gloster aircraft plans for the Russians.
November	*Anti-Comintern Pact signed by Germany and Japan.*

1937

	Many subsequent spies serving with the International Brigade in Spain, where first approaches to them were often made.
	Brian GOOLD-VERSCHOYLE, a former out-out for HARDT and KING, after serving in Spain as a radio operator and criticising OGPU, was lured on to a Soviet ship and disappeared.
	Guy BURGESS probably started working for the RUSSIANS.
February	Percy GLADING passing material from or earlier Woolwich Arsenal to the Russians.
July	HARRY II handed over to Henri ROBINSON.
September	*Stalin's purge of Red Army at its height.*
	Ignace REISS defected and was murdered in Switzerland.
	Defection of KRIVITSKY
November	*Italy joined Anti-Comintern Pact.*
	End of second Five Year Plan.
October	VERNON found guilty of improper possession of documents and fined £50

1938

SPRINGHALL admitted FOOTE's name for Russian

espionage work.

January	GLADING arrested and sentenced to 6 years imprisonment
March	***Germany annexed Austria.***
September	***Germany demanded the cessation of the Sudetenland from Czechoslovakia.***
	Alexander FOOTE recruited for R.I.S. ("Rote Drei" organisation).
	Munich Agreement.
	Robinson WALKER sentenced to 3 years penal servitude for trying to pass Vickers plans to the Russians.

1939

Early	O.C. GREEN began espionage activities.
January	BURGESS went to S.I.S (S.O.E)
February	***The U.K. recognised France.***
March	***Germany annexed Czechoslovakia.***
	John CAIRNCROSS passed information on foreigpolicy to BURGESS.
April	***End of Spanish Civil War.***
	Italy invaded Albania.
May	***Anglo-Polish Treaty signed.***
August	***Russo-German Pact signed.***
	Harry SMOLKA employed in the Ministry of Information (News Dept).
September	***Germany invaded Poland. U.K. declared war. Russians invaded Poland and carved it up with the Germans.***
October	KING convicted and sentenced to 10 years penal servitude.
November	***Russia invaded Finland.***

December	*Russia expelled from League of Nations.*
1940	
January	SPRINGHALL National organiser of C.P.G.B. (until June 1943).
March	*End of Russo-Finnish war.*
	KRIVITSKY visited the U.K.
May	*Germans invaded Holland and Belgium.*
June	*Dunkirk.*
	Russia occupied the Baltic republics.
July	Klaus FUCHS (who had arrived in the U.K. in September 1933) sent to Canada for internment.
	Surrender of France.
1941	
February	N.K.G.B. formed
June	*Germany invaded Russia.*
May	FUCHS working at Birmingham on atomic energy.
	Finland joined the war against Russia.
	KRIVITSKY found shot in a Washington hotel.
October	SMOLKA passing secret information to BURGESS.
December	*Pearl Harbour.*
1942	
January	O.C. Green arrested.
February	KLUGMAN in S.O.E. in charge of agents records.
March	GLADING released from prison.
May	*Twenty years' treaty of alliance between Russia and the United Kingdom.*
April	CAIRNCROSS resigned from the Civil Service.
August	*Germans halted at Stalingrad.*
	FUCHS decided to pass information to the Russians and contacted Jurgen KUCYNSKI
	Churchill visited Moscow.
Late in year	SPRINGHALL active. Contacted Olive Mary

SHEEHAN in Air Ministry.

November	***Allied landings in North Africa.***
December	***Limit of German advance in Russia.***

TREPPER was arrested in Paris and betrayed all members of his organisation to the Germans.

Henri ROBINSON also arrested.

1943

January   ***Last Germans surrendered at Stalingrad.***

SPRINGHALL receiving Air Ministry information from SHEEHAN

April   SPRINGHALL met Ormond Leyton Uren who later provided information on S.O.E.

May   ***Germans cleared out of North Africa.***

June   SPRINGHALL arrested and sentenced to 7 years penal servitude. Expelled from the C.P.

Andrew ROTHSTEIN, a known contact of SPRINGHALL, acting as a go between for the C.P.G.B. and the Russian Embassy.

July   ***Allies invaded Sicily.***

October   Ormond Leyton UREN, associate of SPRINGHALL sentenced to 7 years penal servitude.

November   ***Teheran Conference.***

December   FUCHS left for the USA on atomic energy work. Contacted Harry GOLD on previous instruction from Ursula BEURTON.

1944   Alan NUNN May spying for the GRU in Canada.

March   ***Russians advanced into Rumania.***

FUCHS at Los Alamos

May   MACLEAN in Washington

June   Allies captured Rome.

June   BURGESS joined F.O. (News Department).

September	*Finland ceased fire. Russia declared war on Bulgaria, which then entered the war against Germany. Russo-Bulgarian hostilities ceased after one day.*
October	*Russians entered Germany.*

1945

February	*Yalta Conference.*
April	*Russians took Vienna.*
	Death of Hitler.
May	*Russians took Berlin.*
	V E Day.
June	*Quadripartite declaration on the occupation zones of Germany and Berlin.*
July	*Potsdam Conference.*
	VERNON elected M.P. for Dulwich.
August	*First atomic bomb used against Japan. Russia declared war on Japan.*
	Surrender of Japan.
September	*London Conference of Foreign Ministers.*
	Defection of GOUZENKO
December	*Moscow Conference of Foreign Ministers.*

1946

March	*Churchill's Iron Curtain speech at Fulton.*
	MGB replaced NKGB.
April	*Paris Conference,*
	Allan NUNN MAY arrested and sentenced (in May) to 10 years 'penal servitude.
June	Canadian Royal Commission report published.
July	*Peace Conference (Paris).*
	KING released from prison.
	FUCHS returned to U.K to take up work at Harwell.
October	*End of Peace Conference.*

1947

	FUCHS passing atomic energy information to Russians.
March	***Moscow meeting of Foreign Ministers.***
	UREN released from prison.
	"Soviet wives" held in Russia.
July	FOOTE defected to British in Berlin.
October	Cominform set up.
November -	K.I. set up in Moscow
December	
1948	
January	***Communist coup in Czechoslovakia.***
March	***Brussels Treaty signed.***
	SPRINGHALL released from prison.
June	***Berlin blockade and airlift.***
	GRU removed from K.I.
Summer	***"Peace campaign launched under Cominform auspices".***
November	MACLEAN in Cairo
1949	
	SPRINGHALL rejoined C.P.
April	***NATO Treaty signed.***
May	***Berlin blockade lifted.***
September	***First reported atomic explosion in Russia.***
October	***Central People's Government proclaimed in China.***
1950	
January	William Marshall in Moscow.
March	***Stockholm "Peace" appeal.***
	FUCHS sentenced to 14 years imprisonment
June	***Korean war began.***
August	BURGESS appointed to Washington.
September	***MacArthur advanced beyond 38th parallel.***
October	MACLEAN head of American Department Foreign Office.

November	*Chinese troops in North Korea.*
1951	
February	*U.N. voted China guilty of aggression.*
May	(5th) BURGESS returned to U.K. on recall from Washington. (25th) Flight of BURGESS and MACLEAN.
December	K.I. Dissolved.
1952	
April	*Economic Conference in Moscow.*
June	Marshall arrested in company of Pavel KUZNETSOV. Sentenced to 5 years imprisonment.
December	NUNN MAY released from prison.
1953	
March	*Death of Stalin*
June	*BERIYA arrested.*
July	*Korean armistice signed.*
December	*BERIYA executed.*
1954	
February	*Fall of MALENKOV.*
March	Ajit GUPTA found to be receiving money from the Russians for information from the Indian High Commissioner's office in London. K.G.B set up.
April	PETROV defected.
1955	
July	*Summit Conference at Geneva* *Naval visits.*
August	Report of Australian Royal Commission Espionage published.
September	PETROV's story of BURGESS and MACLEAN published.
October	*Conference of Foreign Ministers at Geneva.*

Index of Names

M

MACARTNEY, Wilfred viii, 26, 68

MACKENZIE, Sir Compton 26

MACLEAN, Donald ix, 20, 42-43, 68, 72, 74-75

MAISKY, Ambassador 38

Malenkov 16, 75

Malik 17

Mao-Tse-Tung 15

Marcel PRENANT. See "M.P"

MARIENBACH, Liddia Mikailovna 41

Marshall, William Martin 45, 74-75

Masaryk, Jan viii, 14

MEREDITH, Frederick 28-29

Molotov 17

MONKLAND, George 26

MOOS, Charlotte 3, 21

Mosley 7

"M.P" 31

MUNDAY, Charles 25

Mussolini, Benito 6, 8

N

"N" 31

Nikolaievich, Victor 41

NUNN May, Alan 40, 73, 75

O

OLDHAM, Ernest 23

ORLOV 21

P

PARLANTI, Conrad 24

PETER. See SPRINGHALL, Douglas Frank

"Mr PETERS" 25. See also HARDT, Paul

"Mr. PETERSON". See HARDT, Paul

Selected Bibliography

Andrew, C. (2009). *The Defence of the Realm: The Authorized History of MI5*. London: Allen Lane The Penguin Press.

Andrew, C. and Gordievsky, O. (1991). *KGB*. New York, NY: HarperPerennial.

Andrew, C. and Mitrokhin, V. (2005). *The Mitrokhin Archive*. London: Allen Lane The Penguin Press.

Fowkes, B. (2013), *Eastern Europe 1945 – 1969*. Oxon & New York: Routledge.

Haslam, J. (2015). *Near and Distant Neighbors*. New York: Farrar Straus Giroux.

Hennessy, P., & Brownfeld, G. (1982). *Britain's Cold War Security Purge: The Origins of Positive Vetting. The Historical Journal*, 25(4), 965-974. Retrieved from http://www.jstor.org/stable/2638644

Philby, K. (1968). *My Silent War*. New York: Grove Press.

Pringle, R. (2006). *Historical dictionary of Russian and Soviet intelligence*. Lanham, Md: Scarecrow Press.

Sudoplatov, P. (1994). *The Memoirs of an Unwanted Witness - A Soviet Spymaster. London:* Littel, Brown and Company

The National Archives, KV2-805. *Information Given by Krivitsky, Walter, J.*

The National Archives. *KV-2-995 Vernon Wilfred Foulton*.

The National Archives. *KV-2-2235 ERnst David Weiss*.

The National Archives. *KV -2-1238 George and Edith Whomack.*

West, N. and Tsarev, O. (1999). *The Crown Jewels*. New Haven and London: Yale University Press.

West, N. (1999). *VENONA The Greatest Secret of the Cold War.* London: HarperCollins.

Volodarsky, B. (2015). *Stalin's agent: the life and death of Alexander Orlov.* Oxford; New York, NY: Oxford University Press.

About the Editor

Kevin Gorman served in the British Army for 25 years. He read history at Birkbeck College, University of London and has a Masters degree in Intelligence and Security Studies at Brunel, London University. He currently works in the City of London.

Editors Notes

1. Jan Masaryk was the Czechoslovakian Foreign Minister in exile during the war, he supposedly committed suicide in March 1948.

2. James C Robertson head of "D' Branch (in charge of investigating Soviet espionage).

3. Courtenay Trevelyan Young was a close friend of Anthony Blunt. He was born 2 August 1914 and died in 1974. Studied at Trinity College, Cambridge. He served in the Intelligence Corps during WW2.

4. By 1956 Ronald (Ronnie) Thomas Reed was an old MI5 hand. He worked for the BBC as a Radioengineer then joined MI5 in 1940 to work on double agent radio transmissions. Reed helped New Zealand setup up the equivalent of MI5. He died in Dulwich, London in 1995.

5. Marcus Lipton Labour Politician who used parliamentary privelege to question Anthony Eden about Kim Philbu being the "Third Man".

6. Commander Leonard Burt, served with MI5 during the war, and then took over Command of Special Branch in 1946. He was responsible for arresting Klaus FUCHS and Alan NUNN MAY.

7. "Wops" Without Papers

8. Englebert Dollfuss, Austrian Statesman assassinated 25 July 1934.

9. The 'Zinoviev letter' fake letter published in the Daily Mail it was blamed for the Labour Party losing the 1924 General election.

10. Raid on the ARCOS (All-Russian Co-operative Society), Ltd, London. SIS (MI6) received intelligence the bank was being used as a cover for subversive activities they passed the information to MI5. The Police raided the bank on the 12 May 1927, this led to a diplomatic row between the UK and Russia.

11. The "Locarno Pact" was signed by Germany in December 1925, in which "they guaranteed to maintain the new post-war boundaries with France and Belgium and to submit to international arbitration any boundary disputes that might arise in the east."

12. ibid

13. Molotov-Ribbentrop Pact 23 August 1939.

14. The Bloomsbury Group or Circle where a group of intellectuals, writers and artists during the 1920s. Some of its members fell under MI5 scrutiny due to their leanings towards Russian propaganda.

15. Alger Hiss was accused of being a Soviet Spy but was convicted for perjury in 1950.

16. This spelling of Rumania was used until the second half of the

20th Century.

17. Soviet wives of British and American subjects were barred from leaving Russia to join their husbands. The Russians later enacted a law forbidding the marriage of Soviet citizens with foreigners.

18. The Federal Republic of Germany (West Germany) was formally created on the 23 May 1949.

19. Chiang-Kai-Shek's was seen as anti-communist and more importantly anti-Soviet.

20. Moscow Centre intercepted letter was probably a VENONA transcript.

21. Lavrenti Pavlovich Beriya one of Stalin's staunchest first Lieutenants and a formidable Intelligence and Security official. He was also a sexual deviant who raped many young women and sent thousands of Russians to Gulags and their deaths.

22. Georgy Maximilianovich Malenkov succeeded Stalin until his removal in Feb 1954. He subsequently retired from politics and died in 1988.

23. "Internationals" collective name given to Soviet agents operating illegally in the west (outside of the Soviet Rezidentura of the host country).

24. Theodore Stepanovich Maly on his return to Moscow was interrogated and apparently confessed to being a double-agent. He was tried and executed on the 20 September 1938. After Stalin's death he was posthumously rehabilitated on the 14 April 1956.

25. Edward Phillips Oppenheim was a Suspense Fiction Novelist in the early part of the 20th Century.

26. Kim Philby.

27. Codename "Friend". Boris Volodarsky in Stalin's Agent: The Life and Death of Alexander Orlov p295 states he "died in confinement Orenburg Province 5 January1942".

28. Codename STRELA ('Arrow") responsible for Kim Philby's recruitment by Arnold "Otto" Deutsch into the NKVD later KGB. Died in Brighton, UK, of Cancer 12 may 1973.

29. HANS also known as ANDREI was Dimitri Aleksandrovich Bystroletov, ke was a leading Soviet Intelligence officer who's portrait made it into the secret 'Memory Room' of The KGB Chief's 1st Directorate.

30. William John Hooper 'Jack' held dual British-Dutch nationality. He was recruited by MI5 as recruiter, then duly sacked after it was discovered he worked for the Abwehr before the war.

31. The League against Imperialism was formed in Brussels in 1927, by the German Communist Willi Münzenberg. It became defunct in 1937 after Communist support fell away.

32. "Miss X" was MI5 Officer Olga Gray B5(b) Section, recruited by Maxwell Knight to infiltrate the Communist organisations operating in the UK.

33. Codenamed 'GOT' Percy Eded GLADING alias R Chochrane, was

according to Boris Volodarsky in Stalin's Agent: The Life and Death of Alexander Orlov p493 was recruited 'in or before June 1934' by Ignati Reif (codename MARR, alias Max Wolisch).

34. King Street, Covent Garden, London was the Headquarters of the Communist Party of Great Britain, it was commonly known by its members as the 'Centre'.

35. Georg HANSEN, was a 24 year old German Communist who was part of Max UNSCHLICHT's (personal friend of Walter KRIVITSKY) GRU network.

36. Eddie CHAPMAN, was a wartime MI6 asset who posed as an Abwehr double agent codename ZIGZAG. See, Ben McIntyre's book Agent Zigzag: A True Story of Nazi Espionage, Love, and Betrayal. The story him an MACARTNEY were flouting was sold to the French newspaper, Etoile du Soir. Both of them were convicted under the Official Secrets Act at Bow Street on 29 March 1946. Previously back in 1937 MACARTNEY published a book called ZigZag (Zigzag , by W. F. R. Macartney, published in London by Victor Gollancz in 1937), no doubt this is where CHAPMAN pinched the codename from?

37. Could be Arthur Lewis HORNER the Welsh Trade Unionist and Communist politician who was a staunch member of the CPGB and a personal friend of Harry Pollitt.

38. Wilfred MACARTNEY, died in London on the 4 November 1970.

39. Mikhail SOKOLOV alias Mikhail Yakovlevitch Weinberg, was sent to the UK in 1932 as a legal representative of ARCOS Engineering Department in the role as Manager.

40. Mikhail KAPTELSEV no doubt was an alias, he was replaced by Aleksei DOSCHENKO, another Russian agent, who did almost exactly the same as KAPTELSEV and made approaching an employee at the Rollston's aircraft factory, Croydon.

41. What MI5 did not know at that time was TREPPER was arrested on his return to Moscow and sentenced to 10 years in the Lubyanka prison. He was released in 1955 and in 1974 emigrated to Poland. He died in Jerusalem in 1982

42. Henri ROBINSON alias BOYEN, Alfred; BUCHER, Albert Gottlieb; MERIAN, Alfred; WEHRIT, Otto; "HARRY"; "LEON"; "LUCIEN", born 8 May 1897 in St Gilles, Brussels, Belgium. Worked as an agent for the GRU, in the early 1930's, prior to that he was a Comintern agent. Death: SS Major Horst Kapkow after being interrogated in 1945 informed British Intelligence that Henri ROBINSON was executed in Berlin in 1943, but it was met with disbelief. His exact demise has never been established.

43. Vernon joined the Royal Navy Reserve in 1916 as a Lieutenant, and rose to the rank of Lieutenant Commander he then transferred to the Royal Air Force after it was formed in 1918, where was given the rank of Major.

44. The "Left Book Club" was a left-wing institution during the 1930s and 40's it was founded by Victor Gollancz, who published Wilfred MACARTNEY's book ZigZag.

45. Major Ismail Gusseynovich AKHMEDOV, Section 4 GRU, responsible for foreign technical military information.

46. LUCIE was Rudolf Roessler who was arrested in 1944 by the Swiss. He provided Stalin and Stavka with strategic intelligence, his sources were German Generals within the highest echelons of the Nazi Party.

47. RADO like TREPPER was sentenced to 10 years in the Lubyanka prison, after Stalin's death he was released in 1954. He returned to his native Hungary and died near Budapest 20 August 1981.

48. Ursula Maria BEURTON codename "SONIA" was the atomic Spy Klaus Fuch's handler. On return to East Germany she joined the Socialist Unity Party of Germany, and was given the job as head of the Capitalist Countries Division in the Central Department of Foreign Information in the Government Information Office, she then later became a Journalist and a writer using the pen name Ruth Werner. She died in Berlin 7 July 2000.

49. Jurgen KUCZYNSKI went back to Germany and renounced his English citizenship. He became a prominent economist and intellectual, who was nominated for the Nobel Prize in Economics on three occasions. He died in Berlin 6 August 1997.

50. In November 1952 Rudolf Slansky along with 13 high-ranking Communist leaders were put on trial (supervised by Soviet advisors) all were accused of being Titoists and Zionists. It was a show trial orchestrated by Stalin and carried out by Klement Gottwald who betrayed Slansky. Slansky was found guilty and hanged on the 3 December 1952.

51. SPRINGHALL apparently went from Beijing to Moscow for throat cancer treatment and died there. His headstone in the Babaoshan Revolutionary Cemetery states that he died on the 2 September 1953.

52. Fuchs was interned in the Jewish refugee internment Camp "L' Cove Fields Quebec.

53. "Harry Gold" born Henrich Golodnitsky was Klaus FUCHS courier and was later convicted of espionage and sentenced to 30 years in prison. The Russians also awarded him with the "Order of the Red Star".

54. This information was obtained from VENONA transcripts and passed to GCHQ.

55. Klaus FUCHS served 9 years and 4 months of his Prison sentence. He was stripped of his British citizenship and on release he emigrated to East Germany. He ingratiated himself into the Socialist Democratic society and died in Berlin 28 January 1988.

56. Lieutenant Pavel ANGELOV GRU rezidentura Ottawa. Three days after Hiroshima NUNN MAY supplied Angelov with a detailed report on the bomb that was dropped including uranium samples. In return ANGELOV gave NUNN MAY a bottle of Whiskey and 200 Canadian Dollars.

57. Colonel Nikolai ZABOTIN, legal GRU rezidentura Ottawa, was awarded the Order of the Red Banner and the Order of the Red Star for the NUNN MAY mission. He was also credited with running at least nineteen agents in his Canadian GRU network.

58. On the 5 September 1945 Igor Sergeyevich GOUZENKO a Cipher clerk in the Russian Embassy in Ottawa defected carrying over 100 documents concerning Russian espionage activities in Canada, including details of the atomic energy leaks. Throughout GOUZENKO's life many attempts were made by the KGB to track him down and liquidate him. However, he died from a heart attack in Mississauga, Canada, June 1982.

59. Alan NUNN MAY died in Cambridge 12 January 2003.

60. The October Club was a Communist student club at Oxford University.

61. In 1952 Vladimir KARMANOV acting as the First Secretary of the Soviet Embassy in Belgrade was expelled from Yugoslavia on spying charges.

62. "Purge Procedure" was a vetting process introduced in 1948 run by MI5 and Special Branch.

63. The "Three Wise Men" Sir Thomas Gardiner, Sir Frederick Leggett, and Mr J W Bowen handled the Civil Service vetting rejection appeals.

64. Victor HAEFNER, was a German pilot during World War One. He joined the Socialist DemocraticParty of Germany in 1918. In 1925 he was convicted and imprisoned for passing military secrets to the Western Powers. In 1942 the Nazi's revoked his citizenship. Haefner died in 1967.

65. According to The Mitrokhin Archive p85, he was given the codename "MOLIÈRE", which was later replaced with "LISZT".

66. John Cairncross died in Herefordshire in 8 October 1995.

67. Indeed it was KLUGMAN who recruited CAIRNCROSS and introduced him to Arnold "Otto" DEUTSCH (STEFAN), the Cambridge Five handler.

68. He was fluent in Serbo-Croat hence his work in Yugoslavia.

69. The Russians gave KLUGMAN the codename "MER".

70. Harry (Hans) Peter SMOLKA died in Vienna on the 4 November 1980.

71. Ivan Ilich BARBANOV, Second Secretary in the Consulate-General, London in 1953. He wa accompanied by his wife Lidiya and daughter Tatyana.

Printed in Poland
by Amazon Fulfillment
Poland Sp. z o.o., Wrocław

52084704R00058